TRYING TO SURVIVE:

IN A HOSTILE HOME AND WORKPLACE

DR. ERIC J. SMITH

Order this book online at www.trafford.com
or email orders@trafford.com

Most Trafford titles are also available at major online book retailers.

Printed in the United States of America.

ISBN: 978-1-4269-6685-9 (sc)
ISBN: 978-1-4269-6686-6 (e)

Trafford rev. 05/17/2011

www.trafford.com

North America & international
toll-free: 1 888 232 4444 (USA & Canada)
phone: 250 383 6864 ♦ fax: 812 355 4082

Dedication

This dissertation is dedicated to my father and mother Ernest and Evelyn Smith. This dissertation is also dedicated to my life mentor Judge Levone Graves and my uncle Leroy Pinckney, who gave me employment opportunities and the drive to want to succeed in life. To Jennifer Johnson, she is my rock, my sword, and my shield. Finally, to the women who provided workplace harassment and interpersonal workplace harassment information, without them volunteering, this dissertation would not be possible.

Acknowledgements

I would like to acknowledge my mentor, Dr. Steve Trovik; he gave me the wisdom and insight to finish this arduous journey. Dr. David Pardo my committee member who provided statistical advice and expertise. Dr. Natasha Billups, my committee member who always at the right moment provided comforting words and support. I would also like to acknowledge Mr. Jack Forrest, CEO of Remington Colleges, Dr. Mike Lanouette, and Dr. Hiram Nall who understood the importance of my research and allowed me use of the facility to proceed. I acknowledge Dr. John Guyton and Dr. Brenda Nelson-Porter who have been my sounding board and Dr. Jeffery Kane of Prostatservices for doing an outstanding job with the analyst. Finally, Ms. Daralyn Wallace my editor who put the final touches on my dissertation.

Table of Contents

List of Tables

Chapter 1: Interpersonal Workplace Harassment

In the United States, in 2008, there were more than 46,000 EEOC complaints of discrimination, harassment, and sexual harassment resulting in over 122 million dollars paid out by employers to EEOC complainants (United States Equal Employment Opportunity Commission [USEEOC], 2009). Since 2005, EEOC complaints of sexual harassment, harassment, and unlawful discharge rose significantly (USEEOC, 2009). In 2006, 84.6% of sexual harassment charges filed with the EEOC was from women (Equal Employment Opportunity Commission [EEOC], 2007).

Interpersonal workplace harassment is a subset of deviant workplace behavior such as spreading malicious rumors, sabotaging equipment, or yelling at specific employees in an organization (Lewis, Coursol, & Wahl, 2002). Interpersonal workplace harassment attacks toward targeted employee increase in intensity over a period of time (Meglich, 2008). Women also experience workplace harassment from male partners when domestic violence spills over into the workplace (Bureau of Justice Statistics [BJS], 2007; Corporate Alliance to End Partner Violence [CAEPV], 2005; Hall-Haynes, 2003; Johnson, 2006; Meltzer, 2002).

Workplace violence, sexual harassment, and interpersonal workplace harassment from supervisors, co-workers, and a group of co-workers were used interchangeably in this study. Harassing male partners, male partners, abusers, harassers were used interchangeably in this study; all fall under the gamut of creating a hostile work environment for women employees. Leadership and co-worker responses from supervisors and peers were used interchangeably in this study.

Chapter 1 provided general background information and presented the problem, purpose, and significance of the study. Chapter 1 also included a description of the appropriateness of the research method and design used to investigate the problem, the scope, and limitations of the study. Chapter 1 concluded with the primary points covered in the study.

Background

In the 1800s, United States government officials, magistrates, and organizational leaders considered domestic violence a private issue between a husband and his wife (Hall-Haynes, 2003). Because of the women's rights movement in the 1920s and 1970s, some government entities recognized domestic violence as a social issue. Since then, the incidence of domestic violence across the United States has reached epidemic proportions (Katula, 2006). The health-related costs of crimes committed by harassing male partners exceed $5 billion each year. More than $4 billion is spent on mental health and medical services, while productivity losses account for more than $1billion (National Center for Injury Prevention and Control [NCIPC], 2003).

In the 1990s, women entered the workplace in large numbers (Hall-Haynes, 2003). The demographics of the workplace changed and so did workplace issues (Swanberg et al., 2006). Employers had to address domestic violence incidents that entered the workplace. Domestic violence incidents from partners affect organizational profitability and efficiency as well as workplace safety (Keashly & Harvey, 2006; Johnson & Indvik, 1999; Meyer, 2004; Reeves & O'Leary-Kelly, 2007; Riger, Staggs, & Schewe, 2004). Workplace harassment from male partners costs organizations $5 billion a year (Johnson & Indvik, 1999). The annual cost of lost productivity is more than $727 million with more than $7 million paid workdays lost per year (NCIPC, 2003). In response to escalating violence in the workplace, the Violence Against Women Act (VAMA) was passed in 2003. VAMA allows women who are victims of domestic abuse to file legal actions against their abusers (Katula, 2006). VAMA also holds employers liable for the safety of employees while they are at work.

Past research has shown that employers responded to workplace harassment from male partners in several ways (Swanberg et al., 2006). Some employers provided different types of workplace assistance, ranging from time off without pay to just listening to the employees' complaints (Swanberg et al., 2006). On the other hand, some women received workplace reprimands from employers that eventually led to loss of employment (Bowlus & Seitz, 2006; Brown et al., 2005; Hall-Haynes, 2003; Meltzer, 2002; Riger et al., 2004; Swanberg et al., 2006, Swanberg, Macke, &

Logan, 2007). Women who received reprimands from supervisors in some cases lost their jobs (Hall-Haynes, 2003).

Some women on the job do experience interpersonal workplace harassment from supervisors and co-workers. Interpersonal workplace harassment includes sex discrimination, sexual harassment, and uncivil work behavior such as yelling, making verbal and physical threats toward targeted employees. Supervisors and co-workers who participated in sex discrimination, sexual harassment and uncivil work behavior acts costs organizations billions of dollars each year as a result of women who filed lawsuits (Meglich, 2008; Pesta, Hrivnak, & Dunegan, 2007).

Little pertinent literature is available to suggest how organizational leaders address workplace harassment incidents from male partners after workplace assistance has been provided (Hall-Haynes, 2003). Little suitable literature is available describing workplace harassment experienced by women from male partners after employers provided workplace assistance (Hall-Haynes, 2003; Katula, 2006). Data to suggesting how interpersonal workplace harassment impact employee performance and productivity is limited (Meglich, 2008).

Problem Statement

The general problem for this study was that interpersonal workplace harassment from supervisors, co-workers, or a group of co-workers, and workplace harassment from male partners threatened women employees' job performance and well-being (Hall-Haynes, 2003; Meglich, 2008). Several exploratory research studies exist on workplace harassment of women employees (Hall-Haynes, 2003; Koziol-Mclain et al., 2006; Swanberg et al., 2006, 2007). The specific problem to this study was that workplace harassment from male partners may relate to women experiencing interpersonal workplace harassment from supervisors, co-workers, or a group of co-workers (Hall-Haynes; 2003). As a result of workplace harassment from male partners and interpersonal workplace harassment from supervisors and peers some women employees are losing their jobs (Hall-Haynes, 2003; Meglich, 2008). Workplace harassment is employment hindrance tactics used by male partners and interpersonal workplace harassment is leadership and co-workers responses from supervisors, co-workers, or a group of co-workers.

The quantitative explanatory correlational research methodology was used in this study to gather testable, statistical data designed to determine if workplace harassment from male partners relate to women experiencing interpersonal workplace harassment from supervisors and peers. The general

3

population group was women who were externally employed and were purposefully selected from externally employed women attending a career college in Harris County, Texas. Leaders might use information contained in this study to promote domestic violence awareness in organizations (Katula, 2006). Organizational leaders may provide employees with training designed to reduce interpersonal workplace harassment incidents toward targeted employees (Meglich, 2008). Organizational leaders may identify employee deviant work behavior that hinders employee's job performance and productivity (Meglich, 2008; Swanberg et al., 2006, 2007).

Purpose of the Study

The purpose of this study was to determine if workplace harassment from male partners relate to interpersonal workplace harassment women experience from supervisors and peers. Workplace harassment is employment hindrance tactics used by male partners and interpersonal workplace harassment is leadership and co-workers responses from supervisors, co-workers, or a group of co-workers. The sample size was 130 purposefully selected women who are externally employed attending a career college in Harris County, Texas.

This study contained a research question, hypotheses pair, and instruments designed to generate ordinal data for appropriate selection of a quantitative research method. The explanatory correlational design was appropriate to the quantitative method because the purpose of this study was to ascertain if variables relate to one another. The purposefully selected women did complete the pre-existing workplace harassment tool survey (USGAO/EWIS, 1998) and the pre-existing interpersonal workplace harassment survey (Meglich, 2008). The two pre-existing surveys were used to collect ordinal data.

Significance of the Study

Although several exploratory research studies exist on workplace harassment and interpersonal workplace harassment in the workplace (Hall-Haynes, 2003; Meglich, 2008; Swanberg et al., 2006, 2007). Determining if workplace harassment relates to interpersonal workplace harassment from supervisors, co-workers, or a group of co-workers was research that no published studies have been identified (Hall-Haynes, 2003; Meglich, 2008; Swanberg et al., 2006, 2007). Researchers have paid considerable attention to the effects of workplace harassment on the physical and mental health of women (Swanberg & Logan, 2005). In recent exploratory studies, researchers focused on women's work and employability (Swanberg & Logan, 2005; Swanberg et al., 2005; Wettersten et al., 2004).

Swanberg et al. (2005, 2006, 2007) focused on employment and the effects of workplace harassment in the workplace. Hall-Haynes (2003) focused on what happened after women disclosed domestic violence incidents to their employers or coworkers. The main purpose of Hall-Haynes' study was to see how employers of women responded to disclosure of domestic violence incidents and what workplace assistance women received following disclosure. Katula (2006) recommended promoting the awareness of domestic violence in the workplace through establishment of workplace policies and creation of a task force, workplace harassment training, and domestic violence education.

Researchers have explored the effects of violence in the workplace from a health perspective and not from an organizational theory perspective (Chronister et al., 2004; Hall-Haynes, 2003; Swanberg et al., 2005, 2006, 2007). Hall-Haynes (2003) and Swanberg et al. (2005) focused on disclosure and what workplace assistance was provided. Meglich (2008) focused on interpersonal workplace harassment from supervisors, co-workers, or a group of co-workers and the gender effects thereof. This study research goal was to determine if workplace harassment such as employment hindrance tactics from male partners relate to interpersonal workplace harassment such as leadership and co-worker responses women experience from supervisors, co-workers, or a group of co-workers.

This study did contribute to the results of the exploratory studies of Hall-Haynes (2003), Meglich (2008), Swanberg et al. (2005, 2006, 2007) by providing organizational leaders and society additional research on workplace harassment women experience from male partners, employer responses, and interpersonal workplace harassment from employees in the workplace. This study did provide employers with information to implement effective workplace policies designed to address diverse issues that affect employee productivity. Increased awareness of types of workplace harassment could possibly save the lives of women, as well as save organizations millions of dollars in lawsuits (CAEPV, 2005; Harland, Harrison, Jones, & Reiter-Palmon, 2005; Katula, 2006; Luthans & Avolio, 2003; Meltzer, 2002; Youssef & Luthans, 2007).

Women throughout in the United States continue to experience harassment from male partners in the workplace (BJSCDB, 2007; Hall-Haynes; 2003). Approximately 40% of working women in the United States report workplace harassment (BJSCDB, 2007; Duffy, Scott, & O'Leary-

Kelly, 2005). Interpersonal workplace harassment from employees on targeted employees will continue to be an organizational issue (Lewis, Coursol, & Wahl, 2002). Organizational leaders should continue to develop intervention strategies designed reduce interpersonal workplace harassment (Meglich, 2008).

Significance of the Study to Leadership

Organizational leaders pay millions of dollars in lawsuit settlements to complainants due to interpersonal workplace incidents each year (Johnson & Indvik, 1999; Meglich, 2008). The Department of Labor Women's Bureau (DLWB) statistics from 2004 indicated that women comprise 47% of the workforce. Yet, more than 70% of organizations do not have a policy addressing domestic violence in the workplace (BLS, 2006; Katula, 2006; Keashly & Harvey, 2006; Johnson & Indvik, 1999; Meyer, 2004; Moe & Bell, 2004; Riger et al., 2004; Swanberg et al., 2005).

The results of this study did provide organizational leaders with information on workplace harassment from male partners by providing additional statistics (Hall-Haynes, 2003; Rafferty & Griffin, 2006; Swanberg et al., 2006; Tucker & Russell, 2004). The results from this study may aid organizational leaders in the development of new workplace policies. Organizational leaders may implement training programs designed to save organizations money, increase profitability and organizational efficiency, promote workplace safety and employee productivity (Keashly & Harvey, 2006; Johnson & Indvik, 1999; Meyer, 2004; NCIPC, 2003; Riger et al., 2004).

Nature of the Study

The methodology selected for the study was a quantitative explanatory correlational design. Explanatory correlational studies were designed to determine relationships between the variables (Neuman, 2006). The psychological effects of interpersonal workplace harassment may restrict respondents from information necessary to meet requirements of more vigorous research methods such as qualitative and mixed method, this is the reason other methods have been rejected. The quantitative method statistically addressed the general and specific research problems in this study.

An explanatory correlational design was appropriate to meeting the research goal of this study. The research goal of this study was to ascertain if variables relate to one another. Experimental and quasi-experimental designs have been considered, but not practical for this study. Conducting long-term, in-depth research was impractical because of respondents' program attendance and duration at the career college. An explanatory correlational design was appropriate because data was collected over a single point in time. Comparison groups were not used nor intervention strategies implemented. For these reasons an ex-post facto designed study was not used.

Workplace harassment from male partners such as employment hindrance tactics and interpersonal workplace harassment such as leadership and co-workers responses from supervisors, co-workers, or a group of co-workers experienced by women were introduced as independent and dependent variables. The purpose of this study was to determine if the independent (workplace harassment) variable relates to dependent (interpersonal workplace harassment) variable. Workplace harassment from male partners and interpersonal workplace harassment from supervisors, co-workers, or a group of co-workers experienced by women were not introduced as predictor and criterion variables. Predictor and criterion variables are used in prediction correlational designed studies (Creswell, 2007; Thorndike & Thorndike-Christ, 2009).

Research Question and Hypotheses Pair

The research question was developed from research recommendations made by Hall-Hayne's (2003) and Meglich's (2008) research studies. Hall-Haynes (2003) recommended further research should be conducted on why some women receive work-related reprimands and lose their jobs after disclosing workplace harassment from their male partners to their supervisors. Meglich's (2008) interpersonal workplace harassment investigation into supervisors, co-workers, or a group of co-workers deviant organizational behavior towards employees they target causes some of those employees to lose their jobs. This research question guides the current study:

1. How does workplace harassment from male partners relate to interpersonal workplace harassment externally employed women experience from supervisors, co-workers, or a group of co-workers at a career college in Harris County, Texas?

The hypothesis pair was formulated to gather statistical data from which correlational inferences were drawn (Creswell, 2007; Thorndike &

Thorndike-Christ, 2009). Ordinal data collected did support or reject the following hypotheses pair:

$H1_0$: Workplace harassment from male partners does not relate to interpersonal workplace harassment externally employed women experience from supervisors, co-workers, or a group of co-workers at a career college in Harris County, Texas.

$H1_A$: Workplace harassment from male partners relate to interpersonal workplace harassment externally employed women experience from supervisors, co-workers, or a group of co-workers at a career college in Harris County, Texas.

Theoretical Framework

The current research falls under the employee performance and workplace relationship issues of organizational leadership. The goal of the study was to ascertain if workplace harassment from male partners relate to interpersonal workplace harassment experienced by women from supervisors, co-workers, or a group of co-workers. The theoretical framework consists of Neuman's systems model (Neuman & Fawcett, 2002), Freire's (1970) dialogical pedagogy theory, and Bandura's (1995) social cognitive theory.

Neuman's systems model. According to the Neuman's systems model, the victims of workplace harassment from male partners in the workplace is a combination of interrelationships of psychological, sociocultural, developmental, and spiritual mechanisms in constant interaction with the environment (Neuman & Fawcett, 2002). Within the model, barriers protect women and organizations from external threats such as workplace harassment from male partners (Hall-Haynes, 2003). These barriers may consist of dependence upon family members and familiar associates, if they are available, for psychological support and childcare needs, or for disclosing workplace harassment to employers about male partners in order to receive support (Neuman & Fawcett, 2002). Organizational leaders use protective barriers such as security guards as an attempt to reduce harassment incidents occurring at the workplace (Hall-Haynes, 2003; Swanberg & Logan, 2005). Organizational leaders' protective barriers include educational programs and violence related training for employees (Katula, 2006). The purpose of these programs is to provide security for the employees at the workplace. The workplace includes the physical space around the establishment and surrounding properties (Hall-Haynes, 2003).

8

Freire's dialogical pedagogy theory. Freire's (1970) dialogical pedagogy theory identifies dialogue as a key factor in learning. According to Freire, the fundamentals to dialogue are communication, critical thinking, and intercommunication. Through intercommunication, employers and employees can provide victims of workplace harassment and interpersonal workplace harassment with a sense of empowerment. Freire (1970) cautioned empowerment is not something that one grants to another; Freire stated, "empowerment is a process of discovery and action through dialectic reflection, which in turn causes critical thinking by allowing the exchange of views and experiences" (p.10). According to Freire, critical thinking stimulates learning. Women in the workplace who are taught to think critically can learn to resist the control tactics used by their male partners (Chronister & McWhirter, 2006).

Bandura's social cognitive theory. Bandura's (1995) social cognitive theory posited human behavior as an energetic and unified interaction between the person and the environment. Bandura (1995) defined "self-efficacy as the belief people have in the ability to exercise control over events that affect their lives" (p.9). Other researchers have come to similar conclusions (Hall-Haynes, 2003; Swanberg et al., 2005). In the case of harassment, the harasser uses various techniques to maintain control and power over the victim in the relationship (Kwesiga, Bell, Pattie, & Moe, 2007; Moe & Bell, 2004; Swanberg et al., 2005).

Convergence. Neuman's systems model, Bandura's social cognitive theory, and Freire's dialogical pedagogy theory converge in the area of empowerment. Bandura (1995) suggested an individual perceives that he or she controls his or her own situation defines empowerment. In the Neuman's systems model, empowerment can influence the individual and even organizations because they are open systems subject to internal and external environmental factors.

Freire's (1970) dialogical pedagogy theory, as used by organizational leaders, can allow the two open systems, individual and organizational, to share ideas and experiences through dialogue amongst coworkers, employers, and/or support services. Organizational leaders through dialogue may empower employees (Freire, 1970). Bandura's (1995) social cognitive theory of self-efficacy can empower women to seek assistance and receive workplace support from employers to stop male partners from harassing them in the workplace.

Freire (1970) defined "critical consciousness as learning to perceive social, political, and economic contradictions and to take action against the oppressive elements of reality" (p.19). Chronister and McWhirter (2006) defined critical consciousness as "becoming more aware of self (identity), others (context), and the relation of self to others (power dynamics) and accordingly gaining a critical understanding of control and responsibility in one's life situations" (p. 153). Hall-Haynes (2003) noted that leaders in some organizations utilize resources to address workplace harassment from male partners. Resources include placing posters on bulletin boards that communicate awareness of the problem and assurances that the workplace is safe and supportive of disclosure of workplace harassment from male partners (Hall-Haynes, 2003).

Workplace harassment. Harassing male partners often use employment hindrance tactics designed to maintain control and delay their victims from going to work (Swanberg et al., 2005). Male partners often harass their victims at work (Chronister, Wettersten, & Brown, 2004). Women may seek support from employers or co-workers regarding incidents of workplace harassment (Brown et al., 2005; Swanberg, Macke, & Logan, 2006).

Although assistance provided by employers can be effective at reducing harassment in the workplace, in some cases women received reprimands from employers, which eventually caused some of these women to lose their jobs (Hall-Haynes, 2003). There is no published research suggesting why this occurs or ascertain if disclosure of workplace harassment relates to work-related reprimands (Hall-Haynes, 2003). Research on workplace harassment is relatively new (Hall-Haynes, 2003). Hall-Hayne's (2003) study was germinal to this study. Hall-Haynes (2003) proposed the relationship between workplace assistance offered by employers and workplace harassment such as employment hindrance tactics experienced by women from male partners is a complex relationship that needs further exploration.

Interpersonal workplace harassment. Research on interpersonal workplace harassment is relatively new (Meglich, 2008). Meglich's (2008) study was germinal to this study. Interpersonal workplace harassment is a form of interpersonal counterproductive workplace behavior between members in the organization (Lewis, Coursol, & Wahl, 2002; Meglich, 2008). Interpersonal workplace harassment can be personal, social, task, or work performance based (Meglich, 2008). Some employees who were victims of interpersonal workplace harassment from supervisors and peers have resigned or got fired from their jobs (Meglich, 2008). This study was an exploration of the opinions of employed women regarding workplace harassment and interpersonal workplace harassment.

Definitions

Disclosure is revealing of information that was previously kept secret (Encarta-Webster, 2005) such as disclosure of workplace harassment from male partners to employers (Hall-Haynes, 2003).

Hope is the determination and motivation to accomplish something, and having a viable plan to accomplish the task (Chronister, Linville, & Palmer, 2008; Norman, Luthans, & Luthans, 2005).

Interpersonal workplace harassment is leadership and co-workers responses from supervisors, co-workers, or a group of co-workers that represents purposeful, ongoing negative behaviors directed at specific employees in the workplace (Meglich, 2008).

Male partner is an intimate or previously intimate individual (Swanberg & Logan, 2005).

Trauma is any workplace event that involves an individual being exposed to an incident in which injury or death is possible and feelings of terror and hopelessness are evoked (Strauser, Lustig, Cogdal, & Uruk, 2006, Swanberg & Logan, 2005).

Workplace harassment is employment hindrance tactics male partners use such as physical, verbal, emotional, economic actions, or threats of actions that influence women at home or in the workplace (Hall-Haynes, 2003; Office of Violence Against Women [OVAW], 2007).

Assumptions

Several assumptions exist for this study. The first assumption was respondents will answer the questions on the pre-existing survey instruments truthfully. Self-reporting as a research practice is widely used and generally accepted (Malhotra, 2004; Swanberg et al., 2006). The second assumption was results of this study were applicable to other large population counties and cities in the United States. Harris County, Texas has a population over two million people and is comparable to large counties and cities across the United States. Harris County, Texas is the fourth largest county in the United States population size.

Scope

This study was explanatory correlational. The investigation determined if workplace harassment such as employment hindrance tactics from male partners related to interpersonal workplace harassment such as leadership and co-worker responses women experience from supervisors, co-workers, or a group of co-workers. The variables related to one another. The study involved a sample of 130 purposefully selected externally employed women attending a career college in Harris County, Texas. The purposefully selected women did complete self-reporting surveys that generated ordinal data.

Limitations

Several limitations exist for this study. The first limitation was women participating in this study who have experienced harassment from male partners may be reluctant to participate in this study because they may be reticent to disclose information about their experiences with harassment. The purpose of the research and the importance of the data collected were explained to the participants.

The second limitation was participants may not answer the questions truthfully. A self-reported approach may contribute to biased reporting of certain behaviors; however, no consensus exists regarding such biases (Malhotra, Kim, & Patil, 2006). Self-reporting as a research practice is widely used and generally accepted (Malhotra, 2004; Swanberg et al., 2006). The third limitation was self-reporting instruments were designed measure women's opinion towards workplace harassment and interpersonal workplace harassment. Prior studies by Hall-Haynes (2003) using the workplace harassment tool and Meglich (2008) using the interpersonal workplace harassment instruments, demonstrated that both self-reporting instruments were practical for measuring workplace harassment and interpersonal workplace harassment among participants.

The fourth limitation was the data added from the study was limited to validity, scope, and reliability of the workplace harassment tool instrument (USGAO/EWIS, 1998) and the interpersonal workplace harassment instrument (Meglich, 2008). Prior literature established reliability of the instruments (Hall-Haynes, 2003; Meglich, 2008). The Cronbach alpha measure of inter-item reliability on both instruments addressed the validity issue (Thorndike & Thorndike-Christ, 2009).

The fifth limitation was an explanatory correlational design can suggest that variables relate to one another (Creswell, 2007). An explanatory correlational design cannot prove that one variable cause a change in another variable (Cooper & Schindler, 2008). An explanatory correlational design did meet the purpose of this study.

Delimitations

The focus of this study was women externally employed who are attending a career college in Harris, County, Texas. Several delimitations exist for this study. The first delimitation was geographic location, workplace harassment and interpersonal workplace harassment incidents occur in organizations throughout the United States. The study did take place in Harris County, Texas. Practically and expediency dictated the choice of geographic limitation. Harris County, Texas is the fourth largest County in population size in the United States and is representative of workplace harassment and interpersonal workplace harassment occurring in the workplace nationwide (TWC, 2009).

The second delimitation was having fewer than 130 respondents as a sample size will not limit the results of the current study. If the sample size is small and not statistically testable in lieu of the size of the population, the results of this study may not be comparable to other populations in counties similar to the size of Harris County, Texas. The third delimitation was quantitative method using an explanatory correlational design to ascertain if variables relate to one another using Pearson correlations analysis was the best selection for analyzing ordinal data (Creswell, 2007). The last delimitation was the characteristics of the study population, the choice of the geographic delimitation will ensure the variables stay linked to the study population. Using a wider geographic scope could alter the data and impact validity of the research findings (Cooper & Schindler, 2008).

Summary

Further research may save organizations millions of dollars and save women's lives (Katula, 2006; Swanberg et al., 2006). Chapter 1 has demonstrated the need to conduct research to determine if workplace harassment such as employment hindrance tactics from male partners relate to interpersonal workplace harassment such as leadership and co-workers responses women experienced from supervisors, co-workers, or a group of co-workers. Another purpose of this chapter was to indicate possible management outcomes for providing workplace assistance, including improved outcomes for women, a safer work environment, and increase employee productivity and performance.

Chapter 1 introduced the concepts of the Neuman systems model and the recognition of women and organizations as open systems (Neuman & Fawcett, 2002), the social cognitive theory of Bandura (1995) regarding self-efficacy and the dialogical pedagogy theory of Freire (1970) which addresses communication between employers and employees in work environments. Key points discussed in Chapter 1 include the problem and purpose statements, significance, and nature of the study, research question with hypotheses, theoretical framework, and definitions. The final sections of the chapter addressed the assumptions, scope, limitations, and delimitations of the study.

Chapter 2 will provide an overview of the literature about workplace harassment, welfare reform acts, employment, employment hindrance tactics used by the harassers. Chapter 2 contains an historical overview that will briefly focus on domestic violence. The final sections of Chapter 2 will address disclosure of workplace harassment to employers, interpersonal workplace harassment, leadership responses, and building self-efficacy in women.

Chapter 2: Review of the Literature

The purpose of this quantitative explanatory correlational study was to determine if workplace harassment from male partners relate to interpersonal workplace harassment women experience from supervisors and peers. The independent variable in this study was workplace harassment women experience from male partners. Workplace harassment used by male partners was employment hindrance tactics (Swanberg et al., 2005, 2006). The dependent variable in this study was interpersonal workplace harassment women experience from supervisors, co-workers, or a group of co-workers. Interpersonal workplace harassment was leadership and co-worker responses (Green & Mitchell, 1979; Hall-Haynes, 2003; Luthans & Avolio, 2003; Meglich, 2008).

Chapter 2 provides a survey of literature, derived from title searches, articles, research documents, and journals on workplace harassment. Chapter 2 contains an historical overview that will briefly focus on workplace harassment and interpersonal workplace harassment. The final sections of the literature review will address the disclosure of workplace harassment to employers, leadership responses and alternatives, building self-efficacy in women, and finally, productivity. The section on current findings will review contemporary trends on workplace assistance provided by employers and workplace harassment experienced by women before and after disclosure. The section on current findings will review interpersonal workplace harassment from supervisors and peers. The chapter will conclude with a summary of the main points covered in the literature review.

Titles Searches, Articles, Research Documents, and Journals

The literature search revealed 47 online peer-reviewed articles from ProQuest and Thompson-Gale PowerSearch databases ranging from 1974 to the present. The literature search produced 71 peer-reviewed articles from 1988 to the present from the online SAGE publications database. The online SAGE publications database was most effective because it contained the most information pertaining to workplace assistance, employment, and employment hindrance tactics. ProQuest was effective for interpersonal workplace harassment, leadership responses, alternatives, and self-efficacy articles. Thompson-Gale PowerSearch database provided a few articles on leadership theories, domestic violence, and workplace assistance, workplace harassment, and employment. Google searches provided 14 government research documents and 19 books. In all, 151 references were used for this study.

The search for literature on interpersonal workplace harassment, workplace assistance, disclosure, and self-efficacy produced a limited amount of scholarly articles. Elements relevant to the current study included leadership styles, leadership influence and alternatives, and domestic violence. Information on workplace harassment, employment, employment hindrance tactics, and welfare reform research as related to domestic violence was narrow in scope. Elements relevant to the current study are organizational theory, organizational behavior, and work environment. Another component relevant to this current study is the Personal Responsibility and Work Opportunity Reconciliation Act of 1996 (PRWORA), which significantly changed the welfare rules (Chronister, 2007).

This literature review contains peer-reviewed articles, reports, studies, and dissertations on the economics of workplace harassment, employment, and employment hindrance tactics of the harasser, domestic violence policies, and the effects of domestic violence in the workplace. The literature review contains two sections: (a) workplace harassment, and (b) interpersonal workplace harassment.

Historical Overview

Workplace harassment. In the 1800s, United States government officials, magistrates, and organizational leaders considered domestic violence a private issue between a husband and his wife (Hall-Haynes,

2003). Because of the women's rights movement in the 1920s and 1970s, some government entities recognized domestic violence as a social issue (Hall-Haynes, 2003). In the 1980s, economic challenges facing the United States convinced legislators to implement welfare reform acts in the 1990s (Nam, 2005). Converting welfare recipients into paid workers has been an ongoing legislative initiative since the late 1960s. The Job Opportunities and Basic Skills (JOBS) program in the Family Support Act (FSA) of 1988 was one of the major legislative initiatives for transitioning welfare recipients to work (Nam, 2005). The JOBS program affected only a small percentage of welfare-reliant women during budget constraints in the early 1990s (Nam, 2005).

Before 1996, unemployed mothers could support themselves and take care of their children under the Aid to Families with Dependent Children (AFDC) program (Brandon & Hogan, 2004). Political pressure from United States citizens to reform welfare programs, including the AFDC, the Personal Responsibility and Work Opportunity Reconciliation Act (PRWORA) was enacted in 1996 (Brandon & Hogan, 2004). One intention of the writers of PRWORA were to discourage long-term welfare dependency on the federal, state, and local governments by encouraging self-sufficiency, which they identified as financial independence from a welfare state through job assistance programs and employment. Another intention of the writers of PRWORA was to promote marriage (Nam, 2005). The writers believed working families with a joint income are less likely to become welfare recipients. Nam (2005) concluded in his research study of PRWORA the promotion of marriage was negligible (2%, N= 713) and the "result was consistent with previous studies showing the marriage promotion provisions of PRWORA have not been successful" (p. 282). Similar studies conducted by Bitler, Gelbach, Williamson-Hoynes, and Zavodny (2004) and Fitzgerald and Ribar (2004) confirmed Nam's (2005) findings.

In order to receive PRWORA benefits, recipients must work or engage in a work-related activity for a minimum of 30 hours a week (Fitzgerald & Ribar, 2004). Qualified recipients could initially receive PRWORA benefits for the maximum of 5 years in their lifetime (Bitler et al., 2004). Although federal government officials composed the basic policy structure and implementation of this act, state legislators retained flexibility over the content of the welfare program, and many state legislators incorporated welfare to work training programs (Nam, 2005).

Before the passage of PRWORA, several factors indicated why women became long-term welfare recipients. Some women suffered from poor physical health (Brandon & Hogan, 2004), some women lacked transportation, and some women experienced posttraumatic stress syndrome (Gorde, Helfrich, & Finlayson, 2004; Woods, 2005). Women's partners served as barriers to work participation (Neuman & Fawcett, 2002; Tolman & Wang, 2005) and economic advancement (Chronister, 2007). Some women stayed on welfare because they could not find a job that paid more than welfare (Lee & Vinokur, 2007).

After passage and implementation of PRWORA, welfare benefit recipients receiving cash assistance dropped 54% from 4.4 million to 2.1 million by 2003 (Dawson & Huntington, 2004). Many unemployed women had to find employment because welfare assistance was no longer an option (Bassuk, Lown, Schmidt, & Wiley, 2006; Cherlin, Burton, Hurt, & Purvin, 2004; Purvin, 2007). After researching welfare reform, Nam (2005) concluded, "segment of welfare recipients, probably the most disadvantaged group left (or were forced to leave) welfare without having the proper means to live" (p. 288).

After passage of PRWORA act of 1996, more women went to work. Domestic violence from male partners spilled over into the workplace (Campbell & Manganello, 2006; Johnson & Indvik, 1999). Advocates against domestic violence helped to increase awareness in communities across the United States and were influential in implementing policies designed to eradicate domestic violence in the workplace (Farmer & Tiefenthaler, 2003). One established principle proven to reduce the effects of domestic violence is gaining independence through financial assistance from employers and government sources (Allen, Bybee, & Sullivan, 2004; Chronister & McWhirter, 2006; Moe & Bell, 2004). Women with children who could not find work within the 5-year unemployment benefits period needed additional financial assistance. Legislators responded by passing the Family Violence Option Act (FVOA).

Legislators made FVOA part of the Temporary Assistance for Needy Families Act (TANF) of 2003 (Lindhorst, Oxford, & Gillmore, 2007). Under TANF, caseworkers could provide women waivers on a case-by-case basis (good cause or grant) to allow them to receive temporary assistance longer than the specified timeframe if they met certain requirements (Lindhorst, Oxford, & Gillmore, 2007). By 2002, 25% of TANF recipients were participating in the labor market compared to 7% in 1992 (Department of Health and Human Services [DHHS], 2004).

Interpersonal workplace harassment. Although abusive behavior such as harassment have been in society for many years, there is increased interest in how these behaviors impact the workplace especially between supervisors and peers (Hunter & Bandow, 2009). In the 1960s, interpersonal workplace harassment incidents between supervisors and peers occurred in every organization throughout the United States (Lewis, Coursol, & Wahl, 2002). Some supervisors and peers negative responses and behavior toward certain employees in organizations caused some of those employees to lose their jobs (Meglich, 2008).

Interpersonal workplace harassment incidents such as sexual harassment, intimidation and workplace violence were underreported because of fear or retaliation and no laws were in place to protect the employee (Meglich, 2008; Hunter & Bandow, 2009). Legislators responded by passing the Civil Right Act of 1964, this federal law afforded legal protection to employees that were victims of interpersonal workplace harassment and discrimination (Lewis, Coursol, & Wahl, 2002). In the 1990s, interpersonal workplace harassment from supervisors and peers received national media coverage from workplace violent acts committed by some disgruntled postal worker employees nationwide (Hunter & Bandow, 2009). Legislators passed several workplace violence acts and organizational leaders nationwide implemented policies against workplace violence (Katula, 2006).

Current Findings

Workplace harassment. Employment and welfare-to-work training programs created a level of independence from harassers (Moe & Bell, 2004). Any level of independence counters the goal of harassers, which is to establish power and control in their relationships with their victims (Moe & Bell, 2004). In effort to regain control in relationships, harassers sometimes increase psychological and physical violence against their victims in order to break down resistance barriers (Koziol-Mclain et al., 2006; Neuman & Fawcett, 2002).

An important factor affecting women's ability to work is how much support they receive from their male partners regarding their employment (Atkinson, Greenstein, & Monahan-Lang, 2005; Wettersten et al., 2004). In an exploratory study of employed women, Wettersten et al. (2004) found 60% of the women received mixed messages about their employment from their male partners. Mixed messages concerning employment were contingent on the harasser's need of the victim's monetary support to ensure household survival and the implementation of control measures designed to maintain power in their relationship (Wettersten et al., 2004). Male partners often use tactics to interfere with the victim's job. Harassers use control tactics to keep their victims dependent upon them, especially women with children (Riger & Staggs, 2004a; Swanberg et al., 2005).

Although women may view work as a haven from their male partner, the level of independence and separation from the male partner that employment brings could also be a source of conflict (Logan & Walker, 2004; Wettersten et al., 2004). The male partner may implement various workplace harassment tactics designed to maintain control of the relationship while the victim is at work, intentionally keeping the victim's attention on the harasser (Brown et al., 2006). Wettersten et al. (2004) found 70% of the women surveyed received harassing phone calls or their harassers made personal appearances at work. As a result, 70% of the women had difficulty concentrating at work, 50% missed days at work, and 60% of the women lost their jobs (Wettersten et al., 2004).

Other studies differ from Wettersten et al. in percentages on the types of workplace harassment experienced by women from male partners. Not allowing the victim to perform job functions or making harassing phone calls ranged from 8% to 75% (Brush, 2003; Taylor & Barush, 2004). Variances in percentages of workplace harassment could be due to the victim's responses to the questions during the research or the questions themselves (Hamby, Sugarman, & Boney-McCoy, 2006; Killas, Simonin, & De Puy, 2005; Romano, 2004).

Employment hindrance tactics. Some of the employment hindrance tactics used by male partners to control women employees include sleep deprivation, destroying work clothing, and stalking (Coulter, 2004; Riger & Staggs, 2004b; Swanberg & Logan, 2005; Taylor & Barush, 2004). Male partners sabotaged work transportation efforts by hiding the car keys so their women will be late for work (Riger et al., 2004; Swanberg & Logan, 2005). Male partners may use physical violence as a tool to hinder their women from going to work (Swanberg et al., 2005).

Cross sectional-studies by Riger et al. (2004) and Leone, Johnson, Cohan, and Lloyd (2004) indicate male partners' employment hindrance tactics ranged from not allowing the victim to go to work or making victims late for work, either of which eventually led to the loss of the job (Riger et al., 2004). Riger et al. (2004) indicate 5% to 27% of the participants lost their jobs because of those employment hindrance tactics. Leone et al. (2004), in a study using low-income women as a sample (N=563), discovered a correlation between the level of physical violence and the likelihood of women missing days at work. For the purpose of this study the items below were employment hindrance tactics used by male partners. The items derived from the workplace harassment tool questionnaire (USGAO/EWIS, 1998).

Employee was harassed at work. The assumption was that item 1 is a component of the independent variable of workplace harassment from male partners and was surveyed as such. The participants did have three choices to make, they circled yes, no, or not applicable.

1. *Employee was harassed over the phone.* The assumption was that item 2 is a component of the independent variable of workplace harassment from male partners and was surveyed as such. The participants did have three choices to make, they circled yes, no or not applicable.
2. *Employee was late for work or left early because of the abuse.* The assumption was that item 3 is a component of the independent variable of workplace harassment from male partners and was surveyed as such. The participants did have three choices to make, they circled yes, no or not applicable.
3. *Employee lost her job because of abuse.* The assumption was that item 4 is a component of the independent variable of workplace harassment from male partners and was surveyed as such. The participants did have three choices to make, they circled yes, no or not applicable.
4. *Employee was discouraged from working.* The assumption was that item 5 is a component of the independent variable of workplace harassment from male partners and was surveyed as such. The participants did have three choices to make, they circled yes, no or not applicable.
5. *Been reprimanded at work for behaviors related to any abuse (IPV).* The assumption was that item 6 is a component of the independent variable of workplace harassment from male partners and was surveyed as such. The participants did have three choices to make, they circled yes, no or not applicable.
6. *Lost a job because of abuse.* The assumption was that item 7 is a component of the independent variable of workplace harassment from male partners and was surveyed as such. The participants did have three choices to make, they circled yes, no or not applicable.
7. *Your partner discouraged you from working.* The assumption was that item 8 is a component of the independent variable of workplace harassment from male partners and was surveyed as such. The participants did have three choices to make, they circled yes, no or not applicable.
8. *Your partner prevented you from working (if yes to question 9 give examples).*

The assumption was that item 9 is a component of the independent variable of work place harassment and was surveyed as such. The participants did will have three choices to make, they circled yes, no or not applicable. The participants did have an opportunity to write down specific examples of workplace harassment from male partners.

Physical violence male partners' use is contingent upon the women's income (Ceballo, Ramirez, Castillo, Caballero, & Lozoff, 2004). Ceballo et al. (2004) found low-income men were more abusive than high income men. Atkinson et al. (2005) argued low-income men are no more abusive than high-income men. Moe and Bell (2004) concluded, although women's specific experiences with abuse as a barrier "to employment were diverse, they all shared the common experience of fearing for their safety, and their efforts to avoid future victimization affected their abilities to work" (p. 45).

Meltzer (2002), on the other hand, argued a stressful work environment might be the cause of domestic violence. Women go home stressed out from work creating an environment ripe for the escalation of violence (Meltzer, 2002). Swanberg et al. (2005) posited there is a limited amount of "information on the employee prevalence of partner violence and its effects on employment and job performance, [and] more specifically information is lacking about the overall prevalence of violence among the general workforce" (p. 19). Only a small percentage of organizations across the United States have policies in place to address domestic violence in the workplace (CAEPV, 2005, 2007). The establishment of these types of policies and programs designed to reduce the effects of harassment in the workplace is relatively new (Swanberg & Logan, 2005). Duffy et al. (2005) posited, "A better understanding of how partner violence affects organizations and employees in the workplace should lead to more effective organizational inventions that will minimize costs and contribute to the overall efforts at reducing partner violence's devastating consequences" (p. 14). More in-depth research is needed on the short and long-term effects of victimization on women's employment (Swanberg et al., 2005).

Disclosure. Factors influencing women's decisions to disclose workplace harassment to their employers include fear of losing their jobs, retaliation, humiliation, denial, pride, and trust (Swanberg et al., 2006). Trust is the basis for conveying confidential information and it has many definitions. Several widely used definitions of trust begin with the discernment or belief that an individual's words are historically associated with his or her deeds (Swanberg et al., 2006). This is recognized as a central precursor or as a constituent of trust itself (Simons, Friedman, Liu, & Mclean, 2007). Schoorman, Mayer and Davis (2007), in their integrative model of organizational trust, defined trust as "the willingness of a party to be vulnerable to the actions of another party, based on expectations the other will perform a particular action important to the trustor, irrespective of the ability to monitor or control the other party" (p.344). For the purpose of this study, the definition of trust according to Schoorman et al. was the best selection, because it is the organizational definition of trust.

A previous study conducted by Hall-Haynes (2003) on disclosure rates indicated that 70.5% of the participants had disclosed harassment versus 29.5% who did not disclose any harassment. Of the 112 women sampled in the research study, 80% of the women lived below the poverty line (Hall-Haynes, 2003). Hall-Haynes concluded threats of violence, stalking, actual violence, or workplace harassment did not statistically influence disclosure rates.

Swanberg et al. (2006) conducted on disclosure rates among women (N=517). Swanberg et al. reported 67% of women told someone about violence versus 33% who did not disclose. Of the percentage of women who disclosed harassment, 72% told their coworkers, 59% informed immediate supervisors, 5.7% informed their supervisor's supervisor, 0.9% informed human resources, and 0.3% informed an employee assistance professional (Swanberg et al., 2006). Women who did not disclose harassment cited the following reasons: embarrassment, fear of judgment or job loss, lack of trust in coworkers, or threats from harassers (Swanberg et al., 2006).

Swanberg et al. (2006) explored the employment aspect of women and developed a matrix using job characteristics, job interference, and workplace consequences as criteria of analysis. Swanberg et al. also noted differences in job tenure, job schedule, hourly wage, and current employment status. Swanberg et al. found women with longer job tenures were more likely to disclose workplace harassment from male partners than women with shorter average job tenure were (2.46 years vs. 1.41 years; $x2$ [493, N=495]; p <.01). Swanberg et al. results indicated that women working full-time in organizations were more likely to disclose workplace harassment from male partners to employers than women working part-time were (80% to 69%; $X2$ [N=497]; p<.01). Swanberg et al. also found that women who disclosed workplace harassment from male partners to employers had an hourly wage of $6 per hour or more (79% vs. 65%; $X2$ [3N=404]).

Workplace assistance. Women frequently are employed in front-line positions such as receptionists, secretaries, nurses, and caseworkers, who can increase their chances of being victims of workplace violence should their male partners enter the workplace. Employers have been slow to respond to the rising incident of domestic violence in the workplace from male partners (Swanberg et al., 2005). As recently as 2005, less than 5% of all United States companies have domestic violence policies (CAEPV, 2005). Organizational leaders are plagued with legal actions and employee problems related to domestic violence (Katula, 2006). The procedures among the companies that do have domestic violence policies and workplace assistance programs vary widely (Katula, 2006). Some employers did not provide workplace assistance after disclosure of workplace harassment from male partners (Hall-Haynes, 2003).

Swanberg et al. (2006) discovered that 96% of the women who disclosed domestic violence incidents to their supervisors or coworkers received workplace assistance. Supervisors and co-workers provided workplace assistance several ways: a listening ear (90%), spending break-time together (62%), increased schedule flexibility (73%), and increased workload flexibility (50%). Hall-Haynes (2003) reported different percentages. Of the 79 women who received workplace assistance, 31.6% received time off with pay, 44.3% received time off without pay, 77.2% received emotional support, 53.16% of the employers advised their employees to take legal action, and 24.5% of the women reported that their employers spoke directly with the harasser (Hall-Haynes, 2003). Although percentages and the types of assistance received differed, Hall-Haynes and Swanberg et al. both posited disclosing harassment incidents to employers was advantageous to the women who requested assistance. Women without workplace assistance from employers are at considerable risk for injury, health, and mental health problems from male partners (Brown et al., 2005; Campbell, Martin, Moracco, Manganello, & Macy, 2006; Koziol-McLain et al., 2006; Logan & Walker, 2004; Swanberg et al., 2005).

Some employers responded negatively to the women's requests for workplace assistance (Swanberg et al., 2006). Instead of employers providing workplace assistance, they eventually terminated the employee's employment with the organization (Avery, Patera, & West, 2006; Hall-Haynes, 2003). Hall-Haynes (2003) discovered after disclosure of workplace harassment from male partners women experienced more work-related problems, such as verbal and written reprimands, than women who did not disclose workplace harassment from male partners. There is no published research suggesting why women receive more work-related reprimands than women who did not disclose (Hall-Haynes, 2003).

Interpersonal workplace harassment. Interpersonal workplace harassment is a form of interpersonal counterproductive workplace behavior between members of the organization (Lewis, Coursol, & Wahl, 2002; Meglich, 2008). Employees that are targets of interpersonal workplace harassment report a gamut of mental and physical complaints that hinder their job performance (Lewis, Coursol, & Wahl, 2002). Some manifestations of interpersonal workplace harassment are threats of termination from supervisors, spreading rumors from supervisors and co-workers, blaming targeted employees for poor job performance from supervisors and co-workers (Meglich, 2008).

Targeted employees endure verbal and physical abuse from supervisors, co-workers, or a group of co-workers (Meglich, 2008). Interpersonal attacks on targeted employees gradually intensify over a period of time (Lewis, Coursol, & Wahl, 2002). Interpersonally harassed employees have a higher rate of absenteeism and employment turnover (Lewis, Coursol, & Wahl, 2002).

Meglich's (2008) interpersonal workplace dynamics survey instrument was used in this study. Leadership and peer responses were types of interpersonal workplace harassment in this study. The items on Meglich's (2008) interpersonal workplace dynamics instrument were the scope of leadership and peers responses. Respondents did circle 'yes or no' to the types of interpersonal workplace harassment from supervisors, co-workers, or a group of co-workers items on the interpersonal workplace harassment survey. The interpersonal workplace dynamics survey also contains 32 questions, 9 point Likert-type scale. The Likert-type scale values are *not severe at all, somewhat severe, moderately severe, quite severe* and *severe as it gets.*

1. *Your supervisor/co-worker/a group of co-workers repeatedly and purposely excludes you from meetings that you need to attend in order to perform your job successfully.* The assumption was that item 1 is a component of the dependent variable of interpersonal workplace harassment from supervisors, co-workers, and a group of co-workers was surveyed as such. The participants circled yes or no and circled choices on the Likert-type scale.

2. *Your supervisor/co-worker/a group of co-workers repeatedly blames you for mistakes for which you are not responsible.* The assumption was that item 2 is a component of the dependent variable interpersonal workplace harassment from supervisors, co-workers, and a group of co-workers was surveyed as such. The participants circled yes or no and circled choices on the Likert-type scale.

3. *Your supervisor/co-worker/a group of co-workers repeatedly yells at you, singles you out for angry outbursts and direct temper tantrums at you for no apparent reason.* The assumption was that item 3 is a component of the dependent variable interpersonal workplace

harassment from supervisors, co-workers, and a group of co-workers was surveyed as such. The participants circled yes or no and circled choices on the Likert-type scale.

4. *Your supervisor repeatedly and unfairly threatens you with termination or other negative job consequences for no apparent reason.* The assumption was that item 4 is a component of the dependent variable interpersonal workplace harassment from supervisors and was surveyed as such. The participants circled yes or no and circled choices on the Likert-type scale.

5. *Your supervisor/co-worker/a group of co-workers repeatedly spreads hateful and malicious rumors about your personal life.* The assumption was that item 5 is a component of the dependent variable interpersonal workplace harassment from supervisors, co-workers, and a group of co-workers was surveyed as such. The participants circled yes or no and circled choices on the Likert-type scale.

6. *Your supervisor /co-worker/a group of co-workers routinely greet you in a pleasant and friendly manner whenever you run into one another during the workday.* The assumption was that item 6 is a component of the dependent variable interpersonal workplace harassment from supervisors, co-workers, and a group of co-workers was surveyed as such. The participants circled yes or no and circled choices on the Likert-type scale.

7. *Your supervisor/co-worker/a group of co-workers repeatedly takes credit for your ideas or results and fails to recognize and acknowledge your contributions.* The assumption was that item 7 is a component of the dependent variable interpersonal workplace harassment from supervisors, co-workers, and a group of co-workers was surveyed as such. The participants circled yes or no and circled choices on the Likert-type scale.

8. *Your supervisor/co-worker/a group of co-workers repeatedly and intentionally sabotages or steals your tools, equipment, supplies or work output.* The assumption was that item 8 is a component of the dependent variable interpersonal workplace harassment from supervisors, co-workers, and a group of co-workers was surveyed as such. The participants circled yes or no and circled choices on the Likert-type scale.

9. *Your supervisor /co-worker/a group of co-workers repeatedly withhold or refuse to provide information that you must have in order to perform your job successfully.* The assumption was that item 9 is a component of the dependent variable of interpersonal

workplace harassment from supervisors, co-workers, and a group of co-workers was surveyed as such. The participants circled yes or no and circled choices on the Likert-type scale.

10. *Your supervisor/co-worker/a group of co-workers repeatedly makes aggressive or intimidating physical gestures such as pushing, slamming objects, finger pointing or glaring towards you.* The assumption was that item 10 is a component of the dependent variable interpersonal workplace harassment from supervisors, co-workers, and a group of co-workers was surveyed as such. The participants circled yes or no and circled choices on the Likert-type scale.

11. *Your supervisor/co-worker/a group of co-workers routinely asks for and acknowledges your input on work-related matters.* The assumption was that item 11 is a component of the dependent variable interpersonal workplace harassment from supervisors, co-workers, and a group of co-workers was surveyed as such. The participants circled yes or no and circled choices on the Likert-type scale.

12. *Your supervisor/co-worker/a group of co-workers repeatedly makes unreasonable work demands of you.* The assumption was that item 12 is a component of the dependent variable interpersonal workplace harassment from supervisors, co-workers, and a group of co-workers was surveyed as such. The participants circled yes or no and circled choices on the Likert-type scale.

Leadership responses and alternatives. Harassed employees can be late for work, miss work, or exhibit substandard work performance because of the employment-hindering tactics used by their harassers (McKean, 2004a; Riger & Staggs, 2004b; Strauser et al., 2006; Swanberg & Logan, 2005; Swanberg et al., 2006). Substandard employee work behaviors do have ramifications (Hall-Haynes, 2003). Green and Mitchell (1979) developed the leadership attributive process model. Green and Mitchell (1979) posited that employee poor work performance contributes negatively to the attributive process in leaders. Leaders focus on the employee's work behaviors rather than the cause of the substandard work behaviors and take disciplinary action (Green & Mitchell, 1979; Hall-Haynes, 2003).

Four leadership styles that integrate with Green's and Mitchell's (1979) leadership attributive process are authoritarian, authentic, transactional, and transformational leadership. Authoritarian leadership uses direction, command, intimidation, and reprimand as the primary mechanisms to influence subordinates' behavior (Pearce, Sims, Cox, & Ball, 2003).

27

Authoritative leaders provide rules for the individual or for the group, supply information on how to accomplish the task, and promise reward for compliance and punishment for disobedience (Pearce, Sims, Cox, & Ball, 2003).

Luthans and Avolio (2003) defined authentic leadership as a process that draws from several positive psychological capacities: greater self-awareness and self-regulated positive behaviors. Authentic leadership in organizational context results in both greater self-awareness and self-regulated positive behaviors on the part of leaders and associates, which fosters self-development (Luthans & Avolio, 2003). Authentic leadership creates a positive work environment.

The main component of authentic leadership is hope (Luthans & Avolio, 2003). The findings of Peterson and Luthans (2003) indicate a positive impact of hope on authentic leadership effectiveness, with results indicating managers with higher hope levels have correspondingly higher performing work teams. Peterson and Luthans noted that leaders' "hope significantly relates to organizations' financial performance ($r = .35$), employee satisfaction ($r = .41$), and employee retention ($r = .37$)" (p. 4). When employers create a work environment that promotes self-awareness and fosters self-development, women become more productive (Hall-Haynes, 2003; Swanberg et al., 2006).

Transactional leadership parallels the equity theory, which is based on an effort-reward employer/employee relationship (Pearce et al., 2003). Pearce et al. (2003) noted individuals attempted to rectify situations if exchange ratios were out of balance. Landy (2007) suggested "individuals are more likely to engage in corrective actions when they perceive negative inequity than when they perceive positive inequity" (p. 10).

Swanberg et al. (2005) indicated organizational leaders must surpass traditional leadership approaches in order to deal effectively with workplace harassment. Scott and Davis (2007) added employees enter organizations with different ideas, ethics, interests, and abilities. According to Politis (2004), transformational leaders increase the followers' range of "needs and wants" (p. 5). Politis (2004) defined transformational leadership "as a process to increase confidence and motivation to obtain performance beyond expectations" (p. 14).

Transformational leadership does have limitations. Transformational leadership is contingent upon a leader's charisma. A highly charismatic leader inspires and motivates employees to achieve beyond organizational expectations (Politis, 2004). Rafferty and Griffin (2006) argued employees might exceed standards not because they are more encouraged or motivated it is because they improved their skills. Houghton and Yoho (2005) identified in their contingency model of leadership that leaders in the time of workplace crisis can motivate employees to perform well in a time of crisis. Leaders can build self-efficacy in employees and provide workplace assistance that reduces the effects of workplace harassment (Chronister, 2007; Stephenson, 2004; Swanberg et al., 2006).

Northouse (2007) asserted that leadership is both an art and a science. Leadership is founded upon theories, principles, skills, and traits, which an individual uses to influence another individual or group of individuals to achieve a common goal. Leaders may employ four leadership styles and still may be inadequate in addressing workplace harassment from male partners in the workplace (Swanberg et al., 2005). Leaders can supplement leadership theories with leadership styles to combat the effects of workplace harassment (Lynham & Chermack, 2006).

Much of the existing theory focuses on effective leadership, and on leadership processes at the individual, group, or organizational level. Graen's (1976) leader-member exchange theory (LMX) is unlike traditional approaches of transactional and transformational leadership, which focus primarily on either the leader or the follower; Graen's LMX (1976) theory focuses on the relationship or interaction between both supervisors and employees and consists of the following stages:

1. During the <u>stranger phase,</u> the supervisor and employee establish a relationship based on the job description (Graen, 1976).
2. During the <u>acquaintance phase,</u> the supervisor begins to test the employee to see if the employee is interested in establishing a work relationship that is higher than a work relationship based on the job description (Graen, 1976).
3. During the <u>mature partnership phase</u>, the supervisor and employee share a high quality level of respect, mutual trust, obligation, confidentiality, and communication with each other (Graen, 1976).

Employer responses to requests for workplace assistance from women may be contingent upon their leadership skills and work relationships with their employees (Hall-Haynes, 2003). Leadership skills and work relationships could be the factors determining why workplace assistance provided by employers varies from organization to organization (Swanberg et al., 2005). Organizational leaders can create comfortable environments where employees can disclose information regarding harassment to organizational leaders without fear of reprisal (Hall-Haynes, 2003; Yoshioka & Choi, 2005).

29

Chronister, Wettersten, and Brown (2004) suggested using Prilleltensky's emancipatory communitarian approach. Prilleltensky's (2002) approach aims to free individuals and communities from cruelty by engaging in research rooted in emancipatory communitarian values such as human diversity, assumptions such as knowledge, and practices such as types of intervention. Knowledge is shared and learned through dialogue between employers and employees (Chronister, Wettersten, & Brown, 2004). Freire's (1970) dialogical pedagogy theory identifies dialogue as a key factor in learning. According to Freire, the fundamentals to dialogue are communication, critical thinking, and intercommunication.

Graen's (1976) LMX theory integrated with Prilleltensky's emancipatory communitarian approach would promote a work environment in which women employees could communicate workplace harassment incidents from male partners to their employers. Graen's (1976) LMX theory does have limitations:

1. If the employee is part of the in-group, that employee gets more support and benefit from the leader.
2. If the employee is part of the out-group, the employee receives less support and less benefit from the leader (Graen, 1976).

It is impossible for every employee to be part of the in-group (Graen, 1976). The personality, culture, biases, and choices of the employer or employee are some of the factors inhibit in-group affiliation (Graen, 1976). Integrating Prilleltensky's emancipatory communitarian approach values like caring and compassion with Graen's LMX theory ensure employees do not have to be part of the in-group to get more support from employers (Chronister, Wettersten, & Brown, 2004). Leaders can build a trust-based relationship and establish effective communications with their employees (Carte, Chidambaram, & Becker, 2006; Denning, 2005; Kirby & Goodpaster, 2007; Stringer, 2006).

Self-efficacy. Negative experiences when seeking help from employers can decrease women's self-efficacy (Hall-Haynes, 2003). Workplace harassment and interpersonal workplace harassment has a negative impact on women's pursuit of personal, professional interests, and goals (Bowlus & Seitz, 2006; Brown et al., 2005; Chronister, 2007; Chronister, Linville, & Palmer, 2008; Chronister & McWhirter, 2003, 2006; Mears & Visher, 2005; Meglich, 2008; Riger et al., 2004). Chronister and McWhirter (2003) suggested one successful tactic toward reducing the effects of domestic violence in the workplace from male partners is to build self-efficacy in their victims by offering career counseling.

Bell (2003) argued reducing the effects of domestic violence in the workplace goes beyond financial support. Bell proposed a conceptual framework that is helpful for employers, researchers, and career counselors in understanding what impact domestic violence has on women's career-related experiences and behaviors. Bell's proposed conceptual framework does not investigate the traumatic symptoms affecting the victims of workplace harassment (Campbell et al., 2006).

Workplace harassment produces traumatic symptoms that affect women in the workplace (Strauser et al., 2006; Williams & Mickelson, 2007). Women also exhibit behaviors such as nervousness, anxiety, guilt, low-self esteem, lack of assertiveness, and lack of career goals and interests (Strauser et al., 2006). Strauser et al. (2006) suggested "increased levels of trauma symptoms negatively affect the three major aspects of the career development process: developmental work personality, vocational identity, and career thoughts" (p. 6). Strauser et al. "found a medium effect size for trauma symptoms, with increased levels of trauma symptoms accounting for 14% and 16% of the variance in the high and low trauma groups" (p. 6). Strauser et al. discovered higher trauma levels caused the victim's career goals, interests, personality, and talents to become more destabilized. Strauser et al. (2006) discovered higher levels of trauma affects employee attendance on the job.

Deprince and Freyd (2004) connected the impact of trauma symptoms from experiences with domestic violence to cognitive functioning of women. Trauma symptoms create a barrier to effective reasoning in victims (Deprince & Freyd, 2004). The results of Deprince's and Freyd's study also suggested trauma experience might damage coding of information, retrieval, and memory in victims.

Although Bandura (1995) indicated self-efficacy expectation may influence women to engage in a particular behavior resistant to adversity; some additional factors to consider:

1. The environment a woman lives in or functions in influences the type and availability of resources promotes self-efficacy (Chronister & McWhirter, 2003; Deprince & Freyd, 2004; Lindley, 2005; McKean, 2004b; Strauser et al., 2006).
2. Gender and ethic differences exist in career decisions of self-efficacy (Albaugh & Nauta, 2005; Chronister & McWhirter, 2004; Davies, Gilboe-Ford, & Hammerton, 2008; Whitaker et al., 2007).
3. Effective intervention strategies in the workplace for women developed must match the perceived needs of the women affected (Constantino, Kim, & Crane, 2005).

4. Leaders must implement a theoretical framework effective in reducing the effects of workplace harassment in the workplace as related to women's career experiences and behavior (Chronister, Linville, & Palmer, 2008; Chronister & McWhirter, 2006).

Bandura (1995) designed social cognitive theory to process career and educational interest formation, identify career and educational choices, and make the best determination regarding career pursuits (Chronister & McWhirter, 2003, 2006). One criticism of Bandura's social cognitive theory is that cultural differences may influence the way self-efficacy is developed and experienced in groups or individuals (Lent, Brown, & Hackett, 1994). Lent et al. (1994) modified an application of Bandura's social cognitive theory and labeled it the social cognitive career theory. Lent et al. designed the social cognitive career theory with the specific purpose of understanding the effects of domestic violence as related to women's career-related experiences and behaviors. Lent et al.'s theory complements Bandura's (1995) social cognitive theory with individual, group, and cultural differences. Bandura (1995) identified environmental, behavioral, and social interaction roles of the person that influence the formation of academic and career thoughts manifest in interests of career goals and career improvement actions.

Bandura (2002) modified the social cognitive theory and posited "although there may be cultural variations in the way in which self-efficacy is developed and experienced, personal self-efficacy is no less relevant to group pursuits than individual pursuits" (p. 7). Lent et al. (1994) identified three factors that indirectly influence the structure and conversion of interests into goals and accomplishment:

1. Environment and proximal appropriate influences, including differential opportunities for task and role model exposure, support for and barriers to engaging in particular activities, cultural and gender role socialization processes;
2. Socioeconomic status, gender, ethnicity, innate abilities, and
3. Learning experiences (p. 10).

One assumption made when applying social cognitive career theory is the individual have a general tendency to feel more confident across domains (Borgen & Lindley, 2003). Chronister and McWhirter (2003, 2006) effectively tested career interventions on small groups of women. The results of the experiment showed significant increases in career search self-efficacy and critical consciousness in the participants (Chronister &

McWhirter, 2003, 2006). Chronister and McWhirter (2003) provided quantitative data and confirmed Borgen and Lindley's assumptions (2003) about the use of the social cognitive career theory as a conceptual framework for career experiences and requirements for women.

Blustein, McWhirter, and Perry (2005) suggested using Prilleltensky's (2002) emancipatory communitarian approach to build self-efficacy in employees in the workplace. Prilleltensky focused on leaders providing information or knowledge can emancipate individuals that are physically or psychologically hindered in the community (Prilleltensky & Nelson, 2002). Prilleltensky's (2002) emancipatory communitarian approach complements Freire's (1970) dialogical pedagogy theory, individuals could be emancipated from adverse situations though communication and knowledge sharing. Using Prilleltensky's emancipatory communitarian approach could help organizational leaders administer social support and counseling services for victims of workplace harassment (Bent-Goodley, 2005; Bhuyan & Senturia, 2005; Campbell & Manganello, 2006; Chronister, 2007; Fowler & Hill, 2004; Goodman & Epstein, 2005; Gondolf, 2005; Yakushko & Chronister, 2005; Yoshioka & Choi, 2005).

Another approach is to build resilience in women who suffer from the effects of workplace harassment in the workplace (Hall-Haynes, 2003). Masten and Reed (2002) define resilience as "adaptation in the face of significant adversity and risk" (p. 2). Women harassed face adversity and risk of injury or death whether at home or work (Diop-Sidibé, Campbell, & Becker, 2006; Riger & Staggs, 2004b). Masten and Reed (2002) discovered resiliency developed in several ways:

1. Enhance the talent within the individual,
2. Remove or at least diminish the risk associated with the situation.
3. Develop the processes dealing with the hazard (p. 12).

Positive thinking actually broadens and even improves the ways people cope with negative events (Luthans, Avolio, Walumbwa, & Li, 2005). Luthans and Jensen (2005) discovered in research of "nurses and workplace outcomes, that hope was correlated with both self-efficacy ($r=.35$) and optimism ($r=.52$)" (p. 3). Norman et al. (2005) discovered in research of "422 Chinese factory workers and supervisory performance data, that hope was significantly related to optimism ($r=.29$) and resiliency ($r=.36$)" (p. 5).

Nelson and Cooper (2007) defined positive organizational behavior (POB) as the "study and application of positively oriented human resource strengths and psychological capacities that can be measured, developed, and effectively managed for performance improvement" (p. 5). The criteria for

POB may improve the outcome of harassed employees by giving them the resilience and optimism to replace negative outcomes such as absenteeism, reduced employee productivity, lack of career goals, with positive outcomes such as increased employee productivity and career goals (Avey, Patera, & West, 2006; Chronister & McWhirter 2006; Luthans & Youssef , 2007a, 2007b; Luthans, Youssef, & Avolio, 2007a, 2007b). Positive outcomes include building hope, optimism, resiliency, and self-efficacy in employees (Chronister et al., 2009; Peterson & Byron, 2008).

Career counselors are trying to create intervention strategies designed to assist women who are victims of workplace harassment in gaining liberty from their harassers (Blustein, McWhirter, & Perry, 2005; Brown et al., 2005; Chronister, 2007). Several significant challenges face career counselors in the creation of effective intervention strategies (Chronister, 2007). Women harassed from male partners do not necessarily follow an uninterrupted, linear pursuit of a career (Blustein, McWhirter, & Perry, 2005; Chronister et al., 2004; Chronister, 2007).

Work environment. Swanberg et al. (2007) suggested employers create a work environment responsive to victims who opt to tell someone at work about their harassment. Although 50% of organizational leaders across the country acknowledge domestic violence issues in the workplace, only 4% of organizations across the United States have domestic violence policies in place (CAPEV, 2005, 2007). Swanberg et al. (2005) posited organizational leaders can create a work environment responsive to interpersonal workplace harassment by developing policies addressing workplace harassment. Katula (2006) suggested organizational leaders can provide education and awareness training for all employees with on-site security to protect employees at work.

Productivity. Harassers reduce productivity while the victims are at work by harassing the victims by phone or making personal appearances (Chronister, 2007; Hall-Haynes, 2003; Leone et al., 2004; Logan, Shannon, Cole, & Swanberg, 2007; Reeves & O'Leary-Kelly, 2007; Swanberg et al., 2007). Reeves and O'Leary-Kelly (2007) reported current victims of domestic violence from male partners reported for work but had difficulty performing. Lifetime victims of domestic violence had challenges with work attendance, but once on the job site, victims were as productive as other employees were (Reeves & O'Leary-Kelly, 2007).

Conclusion

The literature review provided a synopsis of the literature and current research that is relevant to the study of workplace harassment and interpersonal workplace harassment. Theories prevalent in the literature review are leader-member exchange theory (LMX) (Graen, 1976), social cognitive career theory (Lent et al., 1994), and Prilleltensky's (2002) emancipatory communitarian approach. Social cognitive career theory identifies the environmental, behavioral, and social interaction roles of the person that influence the formation of academic interests and career aspirations that manifest in career goals and action (Lent et al., 1994).

Organizational leader responses to workplace harassment and interpersonal workplace harassment incidents occurring in the workplace vary from organization to organization (Swanberg et al., 2005). The stigma associated with male partner harassment may influence workplace assistance for harassed employees (Hall-Haynes, 2003). Harassers often implement psychological and physical abuse tactics designed to limit or control their victims' employment opportunities (Johnson, 2006; Stark, 2006; Swanberg et al., 2005). Workplace assistance offered by employers promotes independence, but this independence may be the source of increased conflict between women and their harassers (Logan & Walker, 2004).

Summary

Hall-Haynes (2003) recommended the relationship between workplace assistance offered by employers and workplace harassment women experienced from male partners is a complex relationship that needs further exploration. Women in some cases received workplace reprimands from supervisors after disclosure of workplace harassment from male partners (Hall-Haynes, 2003). Hall-Haynes recommended further research needs to be conducted on why some women after disclosing workplace harassment from male partners to their supervisors are receiving work-related reprimands. Hall-Haynes (2003) recommendations are the basis for this current study.

Women receiving work-related reprimands after disclosing workplace harassment are basis for the development of the independent variable and led selection of the workplace harassment survey. Employers are exploring ways how to combat organizational interpersonal workplace harassment from supervisors and co-workers, but not enough research has been gathered and analyzed to provide specific direction or guidance (Meglich,

2008; Swanberg et al., 2005). An approach to gathering information about interpersonal workplace harassment is to get the opinions of interpersonal workplace harassment from employees (Meglich, 2008). Obtaining employees opinions about interpersonal workplace harassment is basis for the development of the dependent variable and led to the selection of the interpersonal workplace harassment survey. The research goal of this study was to ascertain if the independent and dependent variables relate to one another.

Research from this current study did provide organizational leaders with information on how to provide effective workplace assistance without possibly escalating interpersonal workplace harassment. Studies such as the one proposed here may help to improve disclosure rates. This is important because research on interpersonal workplace harassment could save organization leaders money; improve leadership skills, while improving employees' performance and productivity.

Chapter 3 contains the research method and design appropriate to the study. The sampling population and procedures for data collection, including how research ethics will be applied using informed consent, confidentiality, and a specific geographical location, are discussed. Chapter 3 will also provide details of the instruments used, with discussions of the measurements of the variables and the internal and external validity of the study as well as an outline of data analysis.

Chapter 3: Method

The purpose of this quantitative explanatory correlational study was to determine if workplace harassment such as employment hindrance tactics from male partners relate to interpersonal workplace harassment such as leadership and co-worker responses women experience from supervisors and peers. Workplace harassment produces various traumatic symptoms among women (Bowlus & Seitz, 2006; Chronister, 2007; Gielen et al., 2006; McCarthy, Felmlee, & Hagan, 2004; Strauser et al., 2006; Swanberg, Logan, & Macke, 2005). Chapter 3 contains the research method and design appropriate to the study. The sampling population and procedures for data collection, including how research ethics was applied using informed consent; confidentiality, and a specific geographical location, are discussed. Chapter 3 will also provide details of the instruments used, with discussions of the measurements of the variables and the internal and external validity of the study as well as an outline of data analysis.

The Research Method

The intent behind the selection of the quantitative methodology in this study was to gather testable, statistical data from participants. Data was collected from respondents was set into categories measuring workplace harassment from male partners and interpersonal workplace harassment experienced by women from supervisors, co-workers, or a group of co-workers. The purpose of this study was to ascertain if the independent variable (workplace harassment) relates to the dependent variable (interpersonal workplace harassment). The quantitative method of determining possible relationships between variables was the appropriate methodology.

Quantitative research may be more familiar to educators today who are trained in experimental research, survey designs, and statistical procedures (Creswell, 2007; Leedy & Ormrod, 2009). Other research methods have been considered, but rejected. Qualitative method focuses on constructivist thought (Creswell, 2007). Qualitative method uses an empirical-analytical, interpretive approach involving research (Creswell) and does not reveal cause-and-effect relationships (Leedy & Ormrod, 2009).

The qualitative method will not accomplish the statistical research goal, which is the rationale for using self-reporting questionnaires designed to generate ordinal data. Qualitative research, according to Poggenpoel (2005), involves an examination and description of an identified occurrence in the field; the purpose of this type of research was to test the hypothesis pair and not elicit understanding. For this reason, a qualitative design was not appropriate.

Other research methodologies were unsuitable for the study. Mixed-methods research involves genuine integration between qualitative and quantitative methods (Bryman, 2007). A mixed-methods design was inappropriate because of the nature of the data and the difficulty in merging analyses of quantitative and qualitative data (Bryman, 2006; Swanberg et al., 2006).

Design Appropriateness

As noted by Cooper and Schindler (2008) more formalized studies contain hypotheses or investigative questions, in contrast to descriptive studies. Formal studies serve a variety of research objectives: (a) descriptions of phenomena or characteristics associated with a subject population (who, what, when, where, and how of a topic; (b) estimates of the proportions of a population have certain characteristics; and (c) the association among variables (Cooper & Schindler, 2008). Quantitative explanatory correlational research design specifically to determine if variables relate to another addresses the research problem. An explanatory correlational design using Pearson product-moment correlation coefficient test of variables was appropriate for statistical analysis of the data collected.

Experimental and quasi-experimental designs have been considered, but not practical for this study. Conducting long-term, in-depth research was impractical because of respondents' program attendance and duration at the career college. The emerging data design was inappropriate for the study since all data collected was immediately analyzed (Creswell, 2007). The qualitative method is the best approach when primary issues are unknown and the research goal is to recognize basic occurrence and specific issues (Leedy & Ormrod, 2009). Consideration of other research designs and method led to the determination that a quantitative explanatory correlational design was the best choice.

Research Question and Hypotheses Pair

The research question was developed from research recommendations made by Hall-Hayne's (2003) and Meglich's (2008) research studies. Hall-Haynes (2003) recommended further research should be conducted on why some women receive work-related reprimands and lose their jobs after disclosing workplace harassment from their male partners to their supervisors. Meglich's (2008) interpersonal workplace harassment investigation into supervisors, co-workers, or a group of co-workers deviant organizational behavior towards employees they target causes some of those employees to lose their jobs. This research question guides the study:

1. How does workplace harassment from male partners relate to interpersonal workplace harassment externally employed women experience from supervisors, co-workers, or a group of co-workers at a career college in Harris County, Texas?

The hypotheses pair was formulated to gather statistical data from which correlational inferences were drawn (Creswell, 2007; Thorndike & Thorndike-Christ, 2009). Ordinal data collected did support or reject the following hypothesis pair:

$H1_0$: Workplace harassment from male partners does not relate to interpersonal workplace harassment externally employed women experience from supervisors, co-workers, or a group of co-workers at a career college in Harris County, Texas.

$H1_A$: Workplace harassment from male partners relates to interpersonal workplace harassment externally employed women experience from supervisors, co-workers, or a group of co-workers at a career college in Harris County, Texas.

Population

A total of 130 women who are attending Remington College were purposefully selected from externally employed women attending Remington College to complete questionnaires as members of the population. The responses to the workplace harassment survey were limited to current male partner relationships. The geography of the population was centralized to contact a representative number of respondents in a small area.

Sampling Frame

The current study sample was women, 18 years of age or older, externally employed attending Remington College in Harris County, Texas. The purposeful sampling method was appropriate for this study. The aim of purposeful sampling was to obtain a sample size representative of the population based on the descriptive criteria of women, 18 years of age or older and externally employed to collect data relevant to this study. A career college located in Harris County, Texas was the best selection for the following reasons:

1. The Chief Academic Officer for all Remington Colleges signed a permission to use premises form that allowed research to be conducted on the property (Appendix A).
2. Remington College contained externally employed women who are employed in Harris County, Texas.
3. Remington College contained externally employed women of different demographics (ethnicity, income, education, and employment status).

A sample size of 130 respondents was deemed sufficient for the purpose of this study based on the finite correlational factors. There are 254 counties in Texas. The Dallas District EEOC office has jurisdiction in 98 surrounding counties. The El Paso Area EEOC Office has jurisdiction in 53 surrounding counties in Texas. The San Antonio EEOC field office has jurisdiction in 66 surrounding counties in Texas. Harris County, Texas is the most populated and one of 37 surrounding counties in the jurisdiction of the Houston District EEOC office (United States Equal Employment Opportunity Commission [USEEOC], 2009). There were more than 10,000 EEOC complaints filed in Texas in 2008 (USEEOC, 2009). The Houston District EEOC received approximately 2,500 complaints in 2008

(Texas Workforce Commission [TWC], 2009). There were approximately 600 EEOC complaints in 2008 in Harris County, Texas (TWC, 2009). One limiting factor may be that these numbers may be underreported. Based on the 2008 EEOC complaint numbers in Harris County, Texas and the elimination of men who composed of 62% of the those complainants, a sample size of 130 women were an appropriate sample size from which inferences can be drawn from the population of employed women 18 years or older.

The sample size of 130 is important for other reasons as well. Having fewer than 100 respondents would limit the results of the study. If the sample size is too small and not statistically testable in lieu of the populations, the results of this study may not be applicable to other populations. The sample size in this study did exceed the sample size of 112 respondents taken from Hall-Haynes's 2003 study conducted in Harris County, Texas. One out of every three women was purposefully sampled from externally employed women who attended Remington College in Harris, Texas.

Informed Consent and Confidentiality

Research ethics involves respecting the rights of participants, honoring research sites visited, and reporting research fully and honestly (Creswell, 2007; Leedy & Ormrod, 2009). The Internal Review Board (IRB) engages in risk assessment and reviews proposed research to analyze its benefits (Cooper & Schindler, 2008). The protection of human subjects confers in the following subsections: (a) informed consent and (b) confidentiality.

Informed consent. One out of every three women who are externally employed who attend Remington College in Harris County, Texas, was asked if she wants to participate in the study. After the respondent verbally agreed to participate in the study, she was taken to a classroom where nine other participants purposefully selected were waiting. The women were briefed on the purpose, nature and their involvement of the research and asked to sign a consent form (Appendixes B and C) before participation and collection of any data began.

The women were briefed that they were eligible to win a $150.00 gift certificate if their number was randomly selected. The contact information of the researcher was given to the women participating in the study. All women participating in this study was age 18 or over by signing the informed consent form verifying their age. Each woman participating in the study was informed her involvement in this study was voluntary. Each woman was informed that she has the right to withdraw from the study at any time without penalty and confidentiality.

Confidentiality. Each woman was briefed on the purpose of the current study and data collected from her participation was used only for the purpose of conducting this research. Each woman was told that the results of the study will be published. The women participating in this study was be numerically coded by the researcher. Names of the respondents, place of employment, names of any supervisor, co-workers, and group of co-workers or male partners was not requested nor used by the researcher in any way to ensure confidentiality. The consent forms with the respondent signatures were locked in a safe and will be destroyed after 3 years.

Individuals at Prostatservices statistical consulting services did have access to coding sheet of survey information for statistical conversion and analysis. Individuals at Prostatservices signed a confidentiality agreement (Appendix D). Once statistical conversion and analysis was completed, individuals at Prostatservices did return all information pertaining to this study to the researcher.

All information including hard copies of informed consent forms, survey information collected and CD with electronic data from this study was placed in a metal safe and locked in a secured area. The electronic data stored on the computer is password protected. No one else did have access to the data. The CD and all information pertaining to this study will be destroyed 3 years after the research was completed.

Geographical Location

The geographical location is Harris County, Texas. Harris County, Texas is the fourth largest populated county in the United States (TWC, 2009). Within the geographical area, the population did consist of purposefully selected women who are externally employed attending Remington College located in Harris County, Texas.

Instrumentation

The Workplace Harassment Tool (USGAO/EWIS, 1998, Appendix E) questionnaire consists of nine questions concerning workplace harassment. The Workplace Harassment instrument did provide quantitative ordinal measures. Numerical values were assigned to the responses as 1 = Yes, 2 = No, and 66 = N/A (not applicable). Question 9 also contains an open-ended question ascertaining employment hindrance tactics used by harassers.

The Interpersonal Workplace Dynamics survey (Meglich, 2008, Appendix F) consists of 32 questions about workplace dynamics this includes interpersonal workplace harassment. The Interpersonal Workplace Dynamics survey did provide quantitative ordinal measures for the variables. There are 32 1=Yes and 2=No questions generating ordinal data. Numerical values were assigned to the responses 1 not at all severe to 9 as severe as it gets. Questions 1 through 12 did provide a measure for supervisor actions toward the employee. Question 13 through 22 did provide a measure for co-worker actions toward the employee. Questions 23 through 32 did provide a measure for a group of co-workers actions toward the employee. Questions 1 through 32 did generate ordinal data from the Likert-type scale. Items 1 through 9 on the workplace harassment tool were specifically combined to establish the independent variable workplace harassment from male partners in this study. Items 1 through 32 on the interpersonal workplace harassment survey were specifically combined to establish the dependent variable interpersonal workplace harassment from supervisors, co-workers, or a group of co-workers in this study.

Both Workplace Harassment Tool questionnaire and Interpersonal Workplace Dynamics survey did collect ordinal data. Both questionnaires are less than 15 years old. The Interpersonal Workplace Dynamics survey contains questions of the respondent's type of work. This could give organizational leaders an indication of where workplace harassment is prevalent in what types of work.

Data Collection

The respondents used paper versions of self-reporting survey instruments. The paper version of the surveys instruments was selected because the survey instruments cannot be uploaded into the computers at the facility for the respondents to use. Paper versions of the self-reporting surveys did establish a physical chain of custody between the data that was collected and the researcher (Creswell, 2007).

Other data collection techniques were considered and rejected. Mailed out surveys have a low response rate and survey items may be misinterpreted (Creswell, 2007; Leedy & Ormrod, 2009). Face-to-face interviews are not appropriate to this study; interviews can be lengthy and time consuming (Cooper & Schindler, 2008; Thorndike & Thorndike-Christ, 2009). Although millions of Americans have e-mail accounts, emailing questionnaires to respondent computers was rejected because the respondents may not complete the surveys in a timely manner (Malhotra, Kim, & Patil, 2006; Swanberg et al., 2006).

The participants did complete the workplace harassment tool and the interpersonal workplace survey instruments. Both surveys instruments did generate ordinal data. The interpersonal workplace harassment survey did also generate demographics data such as (a) age, (b) gender; (c) race, (d) occupational setting; (e) current job title, and (f) total paid work experience. The ordinal and demographic data collected was appropriate to the explanatory correlational design and dissertation problem because the data was statistically analyzed to meet the research goal of this study.

In order to get representation of the population, and to explore the possible relationship between the variables and meet the requirements of this current study, 130 purposefully selected women did complete self-reporting questionnaires. The respondents in this study did complete the Workplace Harassment tool first, and completed the Interpersonal Workplace Dynamic Survey second. Data collection did continue over an undetermined period until the sample size of 130 respondents was achieved. All assessment instruments were offered in English with the assistance of an English interpreter if needed. Once self-reporting surveys were completed, the participants left the classroom through an adjacent exit away from where the other respondents were waiting in the other classroom to participate in the study.

There was a possibility of participants discussing the purpose of this study, which could potentially affect the results. Respondents were instructed not to discuss the contents of the study with other possible participants. If any participant in this study wanted to stop answering questions on the self-reporting surveys during data collection process, all data collected pertaining to that participant was destroyed.

The data collection process lasted about 20 to 30 minutes after respondents were seated and briefed in the classroom. Breaks were given at the participant's request and refreshments were provided. Surveys were read to participants in English at the participant's request. The answers to the questionnaires were written in ink and in English.

Data Analysis

The data collection was completed in its entirety before the data analysis occurs. The data was hand tabulated and coded numerically by the researcher. An independent statistical consulting firm did conduct the data analysis using SPSSv17 for Windows.

The research goal of this quantitative correlational explanatory design study was through statistical analysis ascertain if the variables of workplace harassment and interpersonal workplace harassment relate to one another.

Pearson product-moment correlation coefficient statistically did meet the research goal of this study (Creswell, 2007). Pearson product-moment correlation coefficient did have a two-tailed test of significance; it was based on the wording of the hypothesis pair (Hall-Haynes, 2003; Meglich, 2008; Thorndike & Thorndike-Christ, 2009). Correlational inferences were drawn from yes/no scores taken off the workplace harassment tool and the interpersonal workplace harassment survey. Pearson product-moment correlation coefficient was conducted using SPSSv17 at the .05 level of significance. If the significance value of the Pearson product-moment correlation coefficient is greater than significance set at .05, the null hypothesis tested was accepted. If the significance value is less than significance set at .05, the null hypothesis tested was rejected. Results of Pearson product-moment correlation coefficient were displayed in a correlation matrix. Additional statistical intercorrelational analyses were performed between supervisor, co-worker, and a group of co-workers interpersonal workplace harassment. The variables in this research study were continuous.

The interpersonal workplace harassment survey contains 9-point Likert-type scale items in which respondents can answer 32 questions (Meglich, 2008). Likert-type scale items on the interpersonal workplace harassment survey can produce a substantial amount of ordinal data (Creswell, 2007). The individuals at the statistical consulting firm did conduct analysis of the Likert-type scale responses and converted those responses into descriptive summary statistics in the form of variables (supervisor, co-worker, or a group of co-workers harassment), number of participants, minimum, maximum, mean and standard deviation using SPSSv17 for Windows. The workplace harassment tool contains 9 questions respondents did answer. The ordinal data generated from responses to workplace harassment tool items was put into a chart of frequency distributions by item, category, frequency and percent of non-missing using SPSSv17 also. The basis was to convert large amounts of ordinal data for organizational leaders to view on several pages (Cooper & Schindler, 2008). The descriptive data of age, gender, race, occupational setting, current job title and total paid work experience was converted into descriptive tables and graphs (Creswell, 2007).

Reliability

The purpose of the workplace harassment tool was to assess the level of harassment women experienced from their male partners while employed in the workplace. The Cronbach [alpha] coefficient of the workplace harassment tool (USGAO/EWIS, 1998) was measured as 0.76 (Hall-Haynes, 2003). Harris granted permission to use the instrument (Appendix G).

The purpose of the interpersonal workplace dynamics survey was to assess the gender effects of interpersonal workplace harassment (Meglich, 2008). The interpersonal workplace dynamics survey alpha coefficient was measured at 0.73 (Meglich, 2008). Meglich granted permission to use the instrument (Appendix H).

Validity

Validity is defined by Cooper and Schindler (2008) "as the extent to which differences found with a measuring tool reflect true differences among participants being tested" (p. 235). This establishes criterion-based validity. The validity criterion used must itself be valid (Cooper & Schindler, 2008). For the purpose of the study, the criterion of measurement proposed by Thorndike and Thorndike-Christ (2009) was used. These criteria include: (a) relevance, (b) freedom from bias; (c) reliability, and (d) availability.

Criterion relevancy was applicable in terms of defining and scoring when measuring workplace harassment from male partners and interpersonal workplace harassment experienced by women from supervisors, co-workers, or a group of co-workers. Freedom from researcher bias was reduced when the criterion established gave each externally employed woman at Remington College located in Harris County, Texas, an equal opportunity to participate in the study. The reliability criterion was obtained by using self-reporting instruments in measuring prior workplace harassment and interpersonal workplace harassment studies (Hall-Haynes, 2003; Meglich, 2008). One threat to the validity of this research was the sample of women taken from Remington College in Harris County, Texas, and using the purposeful sampling method may produce results that are not representative of the employed women population of the United States.

Internal validity. One major threat to the internal validity of this research study was the selection of respondents (Creswell, 2007, Gravetter & Wallnau, 2005; Leedy & Ormrod, 2009). If 130 women are not arbitrarily selected, the data collected has a greater chance of not being a creditable representation of the population. Adopting the purposeful sampling method based upon the descriptive criteria addresses this threat. Internal threats to the validity of this study, such as mortality and history, was negligible. The data was collected from participants during a specified period.

Another possible threat to internal validity was the correlational design of the study. Other designs have a higher internal validity level than correlational designed studies. The internal validity of a true experimental and quasi-experimental design is higher than that of a correlational design.

A correlational design has a higher internal validity than a descriptive design (Creswell, 2007).

While each question on the self-reporting questionnaires surely exhibits face validity, evidence of content validity was provided. This study involved the recollection of workplace harassment received and interpersonal workplace harassment experienced by women. The scope of the literature review serves as a support for the content validity in the study. The initial records may exhibit predictive validity and concurrent validity.

External validity. There were four challenges to the external validity of the study. The first challenge to external validity was it will be impossible to generalize the results of the study beyond women participating in the experiment in Harris County, Texas, to women of other demographics and geographical locations across the United States (Creswell, 2007; Leedy & Ormrod, 2009). The second challenge to external validity was some women may experience interpersonal workplace harassment from supervisors, co-workers, or a group of co-workers and decide not to participate in this study (Meglich, 2008).

The third challenge to external validity was the age and external employment of women attending Remington College will allow justifiable inferences be drawn from scores about the population of employed women experiencing workplace harassment in Harris County, Texas (Creswell, 2007). The fourth challenge to external validity was the credibility and trustworthiness of the data collected was based on the respondents' ability to self-report workplace harassment from male partners and interpersonal workplace harassment from supervisors, co-workers, or a group of co-workers. A self-reported approach may contribute to biased reporting of certain behaviors; however, no consensus exists regarding such biases (Malhotra, Kim, & Patil, 2006). Self-reporting as a research practice is widely used and generally accepted (Malhotra, 2004, Swanberg et al., 2006). Participation in this study was voluntary, purposeful sampling based on descriptive criteria continued until 130 or more respondents participated in this study.

Summary

An explanatory correlational design was appropriate for the study because of the selection of the variables (workplace harassment and interpersonal workplace harassment) as a method for answering the research problem through statistical analysis (Creswell, 2007). Precautions were taken to ensure that confidentiality issues did not arise during the research process, which include safeguarding the collected data. The geographical location of Remington College and externally employed women attending Remington College ensured more than 130 women were purposefully sampled in a reasonable amount of time. Data collection using self-reporting instruments and Windows SPSSv17 as a statistical program to perform data analysis was appropriate for this study. The validity of this study including the reliability of self-reporting instruments are described and discussed. Chapter 4 will present the participants' response process, data analysis, and findings of this study.

Chapter 4: Presentation and Analysis of Data

Previous chapters of this quantitative study included details of the purpose and problem of the study. This study contains the history and existing literature surrounding the problem, and the methodology used for data analysis in this study. Chapter 4 includes data collection, the sample categorical demographics characteristics results, descriptive statistics for the items and scales of the interpersonal workplace harassment survey and results of the data analysis in the current study.

Data Collection

One hundred and thirty (N =130) respondents were purposely sampled according to the descriptive criteria in this study. After the respondent verbally agreed to participate in the study, she was taken to a classroom where nine other participants purposefully selected were waiting. The women were briefed on the purpose, nature and their involvement of the research and asked to sign a consent form before participation and collection of any data started. The respondents signed the consent form. The respondents used paper versions of self-reporting survey instruments.

The respondents in this study did complete the Workplace Harassment tool first, and completed the Interpersonal Workplace Dynamic Survey second. Data collection did continue over an undetermined period until the sample size of 130 respondents was achieved. All assessment instruments were offered in English with the assistance of an English interpreter if needed. Once self-reporting surveys were completed, the participants left the classroom through an adjacent exit away from where the other respondents were waiting in the other classroom to participate in the study.

There was a possibility of participants discussing the purpose of this study, which could potentially affect the results. Respondents were instructed not to discuss the contents of the study with other possible participants. If any participant in this study wanted to stop answering questions on the self-reporting surveys during data collection process, all data collected pertaining to that participant was destroyed.

The data collection process lasted about 20 to 30 minutes after respondents were seated and briefed in the classroom. Breaks were given at the participant's request and refreshments were provided. Surveys were read to participants in English at the participant's request. The answers to the questionnaires were written in ink and in English. The participants did complete the workplace harassment tool and the interpersonal workplace survey instruments, not all questions were answered on every survey. Both surveys instruments did generate ordinal data. The interpersonal workplace harassment survey did also generate demographics data such as (a) age, (b) gender, (c) race; (d) occupational setting, (e) current job title, and (f) total paid work experience.

Sample Categorical Demographics Characteristics

The obtained sample consisted of 130 participants. Their mean age was 26.5 years, with a range of 18 to 86 and a standard deviation of 9.3. All participants were female and had worked an average of 66.24 months in their lives (range 2 to 360, standard deviation = 71.22). The frequency distributions of the sample's categorical demographic characteristics are presented in Table 1.

Table 1.

Frequency Distributions of Sample's Categorical Demographic Characteristics

Variable	Category	Frequency	Percent of Non-Missing
Race	Black (non-Hispanic)	55	43.0
	White (non-Hispanic)	15	11.7
	Hispanic	47	36.7
	Asian	3	2.3
	Other	8	6.3
	Total Non-Missing	128	100.0
	Missing	2	
	Total	130	
Occupational Field	Education	32	25.0
	Health Care	26	20.3
	Hospitality	3	2.3
	Manufacturing	3	2.3
	Administrative/Office	20	15.6
	Government	4	3.1
	Other	40	31.3
	Total Non-Missing	128	100.0
	Missing	2	
	Total	130	
Part-time/Full-time	All part	19	15.1
	Almost all part	8	6.3
	Slightly more part	12	9.5
	Equal part	10	7.9
	Slightly more full	7	5.6
	Almost all full	21	16.7
	All full	49	38.9
	Total Non-Missing	126	100.0
	Missing	4	
	Total	130	

The descriptive statistics for the sample on the continuously measured variables in this study, the items and scales of Interpersonal Workplace Harassment Survey (IWHS) are presented in Table 2. Note that for each IWHS item, results are shown only for cases who characterized the behavior described by the item as being an instance of interpersonal workplace harassment. Respondents had an opportunity to assess IWHS items from *1= not severe at all* to *9 = severe as it gets*. To compute the mean score, all scores are summed then divided by the number of scores. If the IWHS mean items was between 4.00 and 6.00, it equaled *moderately severe* on the interpersonal workplace harassment survey.

Table 2.
Descriptive Statistics for the Items and Scales of the Interpersonal Workplace Harassment Survey

Variable	N	Minimum	Maximum	Mean	Std. Deviation
Supervisory Harassment 1	79	1.00	9.00	4.54	2.828
Supervisory Harassment 2	77	1.00	9.00	4.84	2.833
Supervisory Harassment 3	83	1.00	9.00	5.49	2.997
Supervisory Harassment 4	87	1.00	9.00	5.61	3.009
Supervisory Harassment 5	85	1.00	9.00	5.67	3.325
Supervisory Harassment 6	28	1.00	8.00	3.86	2.534
Supervisory Harassment 7	57	1.00	9.00	4.54	2.752
Supervisory Harassment 8	66	1.00	9.00	5.24	3.282
Supervisory Harassment 9	71	1.00	9.00	5.55	3.060
Supervisory Harassment 10	74	1.00	9.00	6.34	3.287
Supervisory Harassment 11	24	1.00	9.00	4.25	2.953
Supervisory Harassment 12	55	1.00	9.00	4.55	2.523
Coworker Harassment 13	111	1.00	9.00	4.77	3.181
Coworker Harassment 14	64	1.00	9.00	5.41	2.827
Coworker Harassment 15	93	1.00	9.00	5.82	2.996
Coworker Harassment 16	29	1.00	9.00	4.86	3.114
Coworker Harassment 17	68	1.00	9.00	5.35	3.001
Coworker Harassment 18	91	1.00	9.00	3.03	2.738
Coworker Harassment 19	113	1.00	9.00	5.01	3.622

Variable	N	Minimum	Maximum	Mean	Std. Deviation
Coworker Harassment 21	80	1.00	9.00	5.63	3.124
Coworker Harassment 22	78	1.00	9.00	5.62	2.929
Group Harassment 23	80	1.00	9.00	5.89	2.960
Group Harassment 24	85	1.00	9.00	6.25	3.158
Group Harassment 25	23	1.00	9.00	4.35	2.442
Group Harassment 26	73	1.00	9.00	5.30	2.797
Group Harassment 27	86	1.00	9.00	6.14	3.003
Group Harassment 28	83	1.00	9.00	5.58	3.073
Group Harassment 29	92	1.00	9.00	6.27	2.875
Group Harassment 30	86	1.00	9.00	5.81	2.784
Group Harassment 31	61	1.00	9.00	5.31	2.796
Group Harassment 32	19	1.00	9.00	3.47	2.816
Mean Supervisory Harassment	110	1.00	9.00	5.11	2.457
Mean Coworker Harassment	121	1.00	9.00	4.73	2.659
Mean Group Harassment	104	1.00	9.00	5.47	2.715
Mean IWHS Score	125	1.00	9.00	4.79	2.520

Individual IWHS mean scores were grouped together by IWHS items: (a) excluded from meetings-SH1, CW17, GH31, (b) blamed for mistakes-SH2, CW20, GH30; (c) angry outbursts-SH3, CW13, GH27, (d) false rumors spread-SH5, CW15, GH29; (e) pleasant greetings-SH6, CW16, GH25, (f) no recognition-SH7, CW14, GH26; (g) sabotaged-SH8, CW21, GH28, (h) information withheld-SH9, CW22, GH23; (i) aggression intimidation-SH10, CW19, GH24, (j) input acknowledged-SH11, CW18, GH32. SH 4, supervisor threatens you with termination or other with negative job consequences and SH 12, your supervisor repeatedly makes unreasonable work demands of you are applicable to supervisors IWHS only.

The descriptive statistics for the sample on the continuously measured variables in this study, the items and scales of Interpersonal Workplace Harassment Survey (IWHS) are presented in Table 3.

Table 3.

Mean scores of interpersonal workplace harassment items from supervisors, co-workers, or a group of co-workers combined

Variables	N	Minimum	Maximum	Mean	Std. Deviation
Excluded from Meetings	100	1.00	9.00	4.97	2.641
Blamed for Mistakes	96	1.00	9.00	5.26	2.521
Angry Outbursts	120	1.00	9.00	4.87	2.944
False Rumors Spread	105	1.00	9.00	5.69	2.834
Pleasant Greetings	42	1.00	8.67	4.13	2.438
No Recognition	85	1.00	9.00	5.10	2.648
Sabotaged	90	1.00	9.00	5.39	3.045
Information Withheld	87	1.00	9.00	5.57	2.790
Aggression Intimidation	118	1.00	9.00	5.12	3.402
Input Acknowledged	94	1.00	9.00	3.05	2.612

The frequency distributions for the dichotomous items in the other measure used in this study – the Male Partner Harassment Survey (Hall-Haynes, 2003)—are reported in Table 4.

Table 4.

Frequency Distributions for Items and Total Score of Male Partner Harassment Survey

Item or Score	Category	Frequency	Percent of Non-Missing
Employed during last 3 months?	Yes	121	96.8
	No	4	3.2
Partner harassed you at work in person?	Yes	19	15.1
	No	107	84.9
Partner harassed you at work by phone?	Yes	35	27.8
	No	91	72.2
Late for work or left early because of partner abuse?	Yes	22	17.5
	No	104	82.5

Item or Score	Category	Frequency	Percent of Non-Missing
Missed work because of partner abuse?	Yes	16	12.8
	No	109	87.2
Reprimanded at work because of behaviors due to partner abuse?	Yes	4	3.2
	No	121	96.0
Lost a job because of partner abuse?	Yes	2	1.6
	No	124	98.4
Discouraged from work by partner?	Yes	29	23.0
	No	97	77.0
*Prevented from working by partner?	Yes	7	5.6
	No	119	94.4
MPHS Total Score	0	3	2.7
	1	65	57.5
	2	14	12.4
	3	12	10.6
	4	7	6.2
	5	6	5.3
	6	4	3.5
	7	2	1.8
	Total Non-Missing	113	100.0
	Missing	17	
	Total	130	

* Provided respondents with an opportunity to provide specific examples

In this research study, twenty two out of 130 respondents were late or had to leave work early due to workplace harassment from their male partners. Thirty five out of 130 respondents received phone calls from their harassing male partners. Twenty nine out of 130 respondents were discouraged from working. Four out of 130 respondents received reprimands from supervisors because of behaviors due to partner abuse.

Two respondents lost their jobs due to workplace harassment from their male partners.

One question on the workplace harassment tool gave respondents an opportunity to provide specific examples regarding male partner harassment. Two respondents had to put make-up on their faces to cover their black eyes before coming to work. One respondent could not come to work because her male partner ripped her clothes off. Another respondent was late to work because her male partner took her car keys.

Research Question and Hypothesis Pair Data Analysis

The data collection was completed in its entirety before the data analysis occurs. The data was hand tabulated and coded numerically by the researcher. An independent statistical consulting firm did conduct the data analysis using SPSSv17 for Windows.

The purpose of the study was to develop a methodology for data analysis to answer the research question and to support or reject the hypothesis pair. The research question was developed from research recommendations made by Hall-Hayne's (2003) and Meglich's (2008) research studies. This research question guides the study:

1. How does workplace harassment from male partners relate to interpersonal workplace harassment externally employed women experience from supervisors, co-workers, or a group of co-workers at a career college in Harris County, Texas?

The hypothesis pair was formulated to gather statistical data from which correlational inferences were drawn (Creswell, 2007; Thorndike & Thorndike-Christ, 2009). Ordinal data collected did support or reject the following hypothesis pair:

$H1_0$: Workplace harassment from male partners does not relate to interpersonal workplace harassment externally employed women experience from supervisors, co-workers, or a group of co-workers at a career college in Harris County, Texas.

$H1_A$: Workplace harassment from male partners relates to interpersonal workplace harassment externally employed women experience from supervisors, co-workers, or a group of co-workers at a career college in Harris County, Texas.

The hypothesis pair was tested using Pearson product-moment correlation coefficient. The coefficient that ranges in value from $r = -1.00$ to $+1.00$ with zero signifying no correlation at all (Creswell, 2007). Pearson product-moment correlation coefficient did have a two-tailed test of significance; it was based on the wording of the hypothesis pair (Hall-Haynes, 2003; Meglich, 2008; Thorndike & Thorndike-Christ, 2009). Pearson product-moment correlation coefficient was conducted using SPSSv17 at the .05 level of significance. If the significance value of the Pearson correlation coefficient test was greater than significance set at .05, the null hypothesis tested was accepted. If the significance value was less than significance set at .05, the null hypothesis tested was rejected. To measure the intercorrelation between the variables supervisor, co-worker, a group of co-workers interpersonal workplace harassment, the significant value had to be less than the significance set at .01. The variables in this research study were continuous. The data analysis related to the current study.

Pearson product-moment correlation coefficient was used to correlate MPHS scores for male partners with IWHS scores for supervisors, co-workers, and groups of co-workers respectively. MPHS scores for male partners were computed by adding all 1= yes responses to items 2-9 (item 1 only assessed working status). IWHS scores for supervisor harassment, co-worker harassment, and group of co-workers harassment were computed by adding the number of 1= yes responses to the questions that assessed if the form of harassment discussed was experienced by the participant. Since the scores are counts, the use of Pearson product-moment correlation coefficient was appropriate in this study. The results of the correlational analyses are indicated in Table 5.

Table 5.

Relationships among Male Partner Harassment, Supervisor Harassment, Co-worker Harassment, and Group of Co-worker Harassment

		Male	Supervisor	Coworker	Group
Male Partner Harassment	Correlation	1.000	.202*	.138	.137
	Sig. (2-tailed)		.032	.144	.148
	N	113.000	113	113	113
Supervisor Harassment	Correlation	.202*	1.000	.635**	.587**
	Sig. (2-tailed)	.032		.000	.000
	N	113	117.000	117	117

Coworker Harassment	Correlation	.138	.635**	1.000	.837**
	Sig. (2-tailed)	.144	.000		.000
	N	113	117	117.000	117
Group of Coworkers Harassment	Correlation	.137	.587**	.837**	1.000
	Sig. (2-tailed)	.148	.000	.000	
	N	113	117	117	117.000

* p < .05
** p < .01

The Pearson product-moment coefficient correlation indicated that the three forms of harassment assessed using the IWHS were significantly correlated. Supervisor harassment was strongly and directly correlated with group of coworkers harassment (r = .587). Coworker and group of coworker harassment were positively correlated as well (r = .837). Supervisor harassment and coworker harassment were also positively correlated (r = .635). The relationships of primary importance in the study were the relationships between supervisor, coworker, and group of coworker harassment and male partner harassment. The results showed that, though coworker harassment and group of coworker harassment were both not statistically significantly correlated with male partner harassment in the sample, supervisor harassment did significantly correlate with male partner harassment in the sample (r = .202). The statistical significance between MPHS and supervisor IWHS supports the rejection of the null hypothesis in this research study.

Summary

One hundred and thirty externally employed women attending a career college in Harris County, Texas was purposely selected to participate in this research study. Each woman signed a consent form before completing the MPHS and IWHS surveys. The mean age for the women was 26.5 years and worked on an average 66.24 months in their lives. Seventy women had next to full or had full-time jobs. The women in this research study were employed in various occupational fields while attending a career college.

Supervisor means score for all IWHS items was 5.11. Co-worker means score for all IWHS items was 4.73. A group of co-workers mean score for all IWHS items was 4.79. The hypothesis pair was tested using the Pearson product-moment correlation coefficient test. MPHS scores were computed by adding the number of 1= yes to items 2-9 and IWHS scores 1 = yes to items 1-32 for supervisors, co-worker, or a group of co-worker harassment. The results in Table 4 indicate that the three forms of workplace harassment assessed using the IWHS were directly and strongly intercorrelated with each other—supervisor harassment, coworker harassment, group of co-workers harassment. The only one of these that statistically significantly varied with male partner harassment was supervisor harassment with a direct relationship between the variables. The statistical significance between MPHS and supervisor IWHS supports the rejection of the null hypothesis in this research study.

Conclusion

The findings indicate that interpersonal workplace harassment from supervisors, co-workers, or a group of co-workers assessed using the IWHS were directly and strongly intercorrelated with each other. There was direct statistical relationship between supervisor interpersonal workplace harassment and workplace harassment from male partners; this supports the rejection of the null hypothesis of this study. Chapter 4 included data collection, the sample categorical demographics characteristics results, descriptive statistics for the items and scales of the interpersonal workplace harassment survey and results of the data analysis in the current study. Chapter 5 includes the relationship to previous research, recommendations to leadership, future research, scope and study limitations, recommendations and summary.

Chapter 5: Conclusions and Recommendations

Chapter 4 included data collection, the results from the sample categorical demographics characteristics, descriptive statistics for the items and scales of the interpersonal workplace harassment survey, and results of the data analysis in the current study. Topics included in Chapter 5 are a discussion about the relationship of the previous research to current research, interpersonal workplace harassment implications, recommendations to leadership, future leadership scope, and limitations of the study, Chapter 5 concludes with recommendations and a summary.

Relationship to Previous Research

Hall-Haynes (2003) recommended the relationship between workplace assistance offered by employers and workplace harassment women experienced from male partners is a complex relationship that needs further exploration. Women in some cases received workplace reprimands from supervisors after disclosure of workplace harassment from male partners (Hall-Haynes, 2003). Hall-Haynes recommended further research needs to be conducted on why some women after disclosing workplace harassment from male partners to their supervisors are receiving work-related reprimands.

Interpersonal workplace harassment is a form of counterproductive interpersonal workplace behavior between members in an organization (Lewis, Coursol, & Wahl, 2002; Meglich, 2008). Meglich also stated that interpersonal workplace harassment can be personal, social, task, or work performance based. Employees that are targets of interpersonal workplace

61

harassment report a gamut of mental and physical complaints that hinder their job performance (Lewis et al., 2002). According to Meglich, some manifestations of interpersonal workplace harassment include threats of termination from supervisors, false rumors spread by supervisors and co-workers, use of anger and intimidation, and exclusion from meetings and sabotage. Meglich also recommended that exploration in interpersonal workplace harassment from supervisors, co-workers, or a group of co-workers continues because interpersonal workplace harassment is relatively new.

The relationship to previous studies conducted by Hall-Haynes (2003) and Meglich (2008) was based on further exploration of workplace harassment and interpersonal workplace harassment. The purpose of this research study was to determine if the variables workplace harassment from male partners relate to interpersonal workplace harassment from supervisors, co-workers, or a group of co-workers. The findings from this research study suggest there is a relationship of statistical significance between workplace harassment from male partners and the interpersonal workplace harassment women experience from supervisors, not co-workers, and a group of co-workers. Although interpersonal workplace harassment from co-workers and a group of co-workers does not relate to workplace harassment from male partners of statistical significance, co-worker and a group of co-worker interpersonal harassment strongly intercorrelated with supervisor interpersonal harassment.

Implications to Leadership

In the Neuman's systems model, women interact with the environment (Neuman & Fawcett, 2002). Within the model, barriers protect women and organizations from external threats such as workplace harassment from male partners (Hall-Haynes, 2003). Supervisors, co-workers, or a group of co-workers who exclude workplace-harassed employees from meetings or sabotage their equipment create a hostile environment for those employees and aid in the breakdown of the affected employee's protection barriers.

Freire's (1970) dialogical pedagogy theory identifies dialogue as a key factor in learning. According to Freire, the fundamentals to dialogue are communication, critical thinking, and intercommunication. Exclusion from meetings reduces organizational communication and intercommunication while making the workplace-harassed employee less effective as an organizational employee. Interpersonally harassed employees may quit or get fired from their jobs, increasing employee turnover and organizational training costs (Meglich, 2008).

Bandura's (1995) social cognitive theory posited human behavior as an energetic and unified interaction between the person and the environment. Women in this research study did experience interpersonal workplace harassment such as angry outbursts (m=4.87), intimidation (m=5.12), or having false rumors spread about them (m=5.69). These interpersonal workplace harassment items would limit interaction between targeted employees and the employees who demonstrate these behaviors.

Implications regarding supervisors. The findings from this research study suggest there is a relationship of statistical significance between workplace harassment from male partners and the interpersonal workplace harassment women experience from supervisors. The most important factor influencing employee training and development is the supervisor in the workplace (Partnership for Public Service, 2007). Supervisory training and development include methods of influencing subordinates' workplace behaviors (Katula, 2006). Supervisors who exclude workplace-harassed employees from meetings or sabotage their equipment will likely demonstrate the same interpersonal workplace behaviors in front of other employees. Through vicarious learning or communication, some employees will modify their workplace behavior to mimic the workplace behavior of their supervisors toward the harassed employees. Although interpersonal workplace harassment from co-workers and a group of co-workers does not relate to workplace harassment from male partners of statistical significance, co-worker and a group of co-worker interpersonal harassment strongly intercorrelated with supervisor interpersonal harassment.

The findings of this study concluded that women enrolled at a career college and externally employed in Harris County, Texas and who are subject to workplace harassment from male partners are significantly more likely to perceive that interpersonal workplace harassment is directed toward them by their supervisors. Women who participated in this study were threatened by their supervisors with termination and other negative job consequences (n=87, m=5.61). Supervisors also made unreasonable work demands (n=55, m=4.55).

Recommendations to Leadership

The Department of Labor Women's Bureau (DLWB) statistics from 2004 indicated that women comprise 47% of the workforce. Diverse workforces in organizations manifest diverse organizational challenges. Green and Mitchell (1979) posited that poor work performance by employees contributes negatively to the attributive process in leaders. Leaders focus on the employees' work behaviors rather than the cause of the substandard work behaviors and take disciplinary action (Green & Mitchell, 1979; Hall-Haynes, 2003). When domestic violence spills over into the workplace, supervisors must focus on the cause of the substandard work behavior rather than the work behavior.

Swanberg and Logan (2007) suggested that organizational leaders do understand the consequences of domestic violence on women's employment. Katula (2006) proposed that domestic violence training occur in the workplace to combat the effects of domestic violence on those affected employees. However, domestic violence training is inadequate as a defense against interpersonal workplace harassment from supervisors, co-workers, or a group of co-workers. There needs to be interpersonal workplace harassment training for employees as part of new employee orientation and annual in-service training. The interpersonal workplace harassment training should include explaining interpersonal workplace harassment, its effects on targeted employees, and establishing an organizational stance of zero tolerance on interpersonal workplace harassment occurring in the workplace. All employees should receive a combination of domestic violence awareness training and interpersonal workplace harassment training along with workplace violence training. This combination training could be called workplace diversity training. Workplace harassment and interpersonal workplace harassment are diverse issues that affect the workplace.

Because supervisors typically interact with employees on a daily basis and influence employees' behavior in the workplace, there must be advanced workplace diversity training for supervisors. Supervisors should receive additional training in workplace harassment identification, employee communication training, human interactions training, and understanding the fundamentals needed to create a positive organizational environment (Luthans & Youssef, 2007a, 2007b; Nelson & Cooper, 2007). Workplace diversity training can build resiliency and self-efficacy in workplace-harassed women and give them the strength to reinforce their protective barriers against workplace harassment from male partners (Chronister et al., 2009; Neuman & Fawcett, 2002; Peterson & Byron, 2008).

Future Research

This research was designed as a quantitative explanatory correlational study. Before this study, there was no published study researching the relationship between workplace harassment from male partners and the interpersonal workplace harassment that women experience from supervisors, co-workers, or a group of co-workers. Additional research needs to be conducted investigating this relationship. This research study was gender specific with males as partners using females as respondents only; future research should explore the relationship between the variables using females as partners and males as respondents only.

Future research on interpersonal workplace harassment should include a qualitative element. Including a qualitative element might provide explanations for the responses given in the quantitative measurement and elaborate on the descriptive statistic items that were found not to be correlated significantly. A qualitative element might provide supplementary insights about employee perceptions on interpersonal workplace harassment not found in the quantitative measurement. Conducting future research on a large chain organization that operates across the United States might increase the significance of the results and provide additional insights about widespread issues of workplace harassment and interpersonal workplace harassment.

Scope and Study Limitations

The research participants were 130 externally employed women attending a career college in Harris County, Texas. The participants were selected using a purposeful sampling method, once selected; they agreed to complete the workplace harassment and interpersonal workplace harassment surveys voluntarily. Participant age, occupation, paid work experiences, and position in their organizations varied.

The first limitation was participants might not answer the questions truthfully. A self-reported approach may contribute to biased reporting of certain behaviors; however, no consensus exists regarding such biases (Malhotra, Kim, & Patil, 2006). Self-reporting as a research practice is widely used and generally accepted (Malhotra, 2004; Swanberg et al., 2006). The second limitation was that the self-reporting instruments were designed to measure women's opinions towards workplace harassment and interpersonal workplace harassment. The study included a Likert-type format for the interpersonal workplace harassment survey. The respondents' understanding of the options on the scale might have varied based on how individuals applied meaning to each option. Differences in understanding could have led to variances in responses. Prior studies by Hall-Haynes (2003) using the workplace harassment tool, and by Meglich (2008) using the interpersonal workplace harassment instruments, demonstrated that both self-reporting instruments were practical for measuring workplace harassment and interpersonal workplace harassment among participants. The third limitation is that the study included generalized findings from women who are both externally employed and attending a career college in Harris County, Texas. Different geographical locations with different respondents may produce different findings.

Recommendations

Swanberg et al. (2006) reported that 67% of the women in their study (N=517) did tell someone in the workplace about male partner workplace harassment. Fear of judgment, loss of job, lack of trust in co-workers, and threats from harassers were the reasons why 33% did not disclose such information (Swanberg et al., 2006). The findings from this research study suggest there is a direct relationship between workplace harassment from male partners and interpersonal workplace harassment from supervisors. Supervisor interpersonal workplace harassment intercorrelated with co-workers and a group of co-workers interpersonal harassment. Workplace diversity training programs may reduce interpersonal workplace harassment in the workplace and create an environment based on trust where more women can disclose workplace harassment.

Workplace harassment affects employee productivity and attendance (Reeves & O'Leary-Kelly, 2007). Interpersonal workplace harassment affects employee productivity and turnover (Meglich, 2008). The findings from this research study conclude some women are experiencing a hostile environment at home and in the workplace. Workplace assistance from leaders and co-workers in organizations were instrumental in women leaving their harassers (Hall-Haynes, 2003).

Summary

The quantitative explanatory correlational research study included the examination of the relationship between workplace harassment from male partners and interpersonal workplace harassment from supervisors, co-workers, and a group of co-workers. The findings from this research study suggest there is a relationship of statistical significance between workplace harassment from male partners and the interpersonal workplace harassment women experience from supervisors, not co-workers, or a group of co-workers. Although interpersonal workplace harassment from co-workers and a group of co-workers does not relate to workplace harassment from male partners of statistical significance, co-worker and a group of co-worker interpersonal harassment strongly intercorrelated with supervisor interpersonal harassment.

There needs to be interpersonal workplace harassment training for employees as part of new employee orientation and annual in-service training. The interpersonal workplace harassment training should include explanations of interpersonal workplace harassment, the effects of interpersonal workplace harassment on targeted employees, and training regarding the organizational stance of zero tolerance on interpersonal workplace harassment occurring in the workplace. All employees should receive a combination of domestic violence awareness training and interpersonal workplace harassment training along with workplace violence training. The combination training can be called workplace diversity training.

There must be advanced workplace diversity training for supervisors. Supervisors should receive additional training in identification of workplace harassment, employee communications, human interactions, and understanding the fundamentals needed to create a positive organizational environment (Luthans & Youssef, 2007a, 2007b; Nelson & Cooper, 2007). Workplace diversity training can build resiliency and self-efficacy in workplace-harassed women and give them the strength to reinforce their protective barriers against workplace harassment from male partners (Chronister et al., 2009; Neuman & Fawcett, 2002; Peterson & Byron, 2008). Before this study, there was no published study researching the relationship between workplace harassment from male partners and the interpersonal workplace harassment that women experience from supervisors, co-workers, and a group of co-workers. Future research needs to be conducted investigating this relationship.

Conclusion

Workplace harassment from male partners and interpersonal workplace harassment from supervisors, co-workers, or a group of co-workers will continue occurring in the workplace. What is important is how leaders respond to workplace harassment and interpersonal workplace harassment occurrences. There are significant organizational challenges between providing support and the appearance of showing favoritism toward workplace harassed employees. The appearance of showing favoritism toward any employee can create an hostile environment. What is key is having information which provides flexibility to make positive decisions to meet organizational challenges. It is imperative to have training such as workplace diversity training to address diverse issues affecting employees in the workplace.

References

Albaugh, L. M., & Nauta, M., M. (2005). Career decision self-efficacy, career barriers, and college women's experiences of intimate partner violence. *Journal of Career Assessment, 13,* 288-306.

Allen, N., Bybee, D., & Sullivan, C. (2004). Battered women's multiple needs. *Violence Against Women,10,* 1015-1035.

Atkinson, M. P., Greenstein, T, N., & Monahan-Lang, M. (2005). For women, breadwinning can be dangerous: Gendered resource theory and wife abuse. *Journal of Marriage and Family, 67*(5), 1137-1149.

Avey, J. B., Patera, J., & West, B. J. (2006). The implications of positive psychological capital on employee absenteeism. *Journal of Leadership and Organizational studies, 12,* 1-18.

Bandura, A. (1995). *Exercise of personal and collective efficacy.* New York: Cambridge University Press.

Bandura, A. (2002). Social cognitive theory in cultural context. *Applied Psychology: An International Review, 51,* 269-290.

Bassuk, S., Lown, A., Schmidt, L., & Wiley, J. (2006). Interpersonal violence among women seeking welfare: Unraveling lives. *American Journal of Public Health, 96,* 1409-1415.

Bell, H. (2003). Cycles within cycles: Domestic violence, welfare, and low-wage work. *Violence Against Women, 9,* 1245-1262.

Bent-Goodley, T. B. (2005). Culture and domestic violence: Transforming knowledge development. *Journal of Interpersonal Violence, 20*(2), 195-203.

Bhuyan, R., & Senturia, K. (2005). Understanding domestic violence resource utilization and survivor solutions among immigrant and refugee women: Introduction to the special issue. *Journal of Interpersonal Violence, 20*(8), 895-901.

Bitler, M., Gelbach, J. B., Williamson-Hoynes, H., & Zavodny, M. (2004). The impact of welfare reform on marriage and divorce. *Demography, 41*(2), 213-236.

Blustein, D. L., McWhirter, E. H., & Perry, J. C. (2005). Toward an emancipatory communitarian approach to vocational development theory: Research and practice. *The Counseling Psychologist, 33,* 141-179.

Borgen, F. H., & Lindley, L. D. (2003). Individuality and optimal human functioning: Interests, self-efficacy, and personality. In W. B. Walsh (Ed.), *Counseling psychology and optimal human functioning* (pp.55-91). Mahwah, NJ: Lawrence Erlbaum.

Bowlus, A. J., & Seitz, S. N. (2006). Domestic violence, employment, and divorce. *International Economic Review, 47*(4), 1113-1149.

Brandon, P. D., & Hogan, D. P. (2004). Impediments to mothers leaving welfare: The role of maternal and child disability. *Population Research and Policy Review, 23*(4), 419-436.

Brown, C., Linnemeyer, R. M., Dougherty, W. L., Coulson, J. C., Trangsrud, H. B., & Farnsworth, I. V. (2005). Battered women's process of leaving: Implications for career counseling. *Journal of Career Assessment, 13*(4), 452-475.

Brush, L. D. (2003). Effects of work on hitting and hurting. *Violence Against Women, 9,* 1213-1230.

Bryman, A. (2006). Integrating quantitative and qualitative research: How is it done? *Qualitative Research, 6,* 97-113.

Bryman, A. (2007). Barriers to integrating quantitative and qualitative research. *Journal of Mixed Methods Research, 1(8),* 1-16.

Bureau of Justice Statistics. (2007). *Intimate partner violence in the United States 1993-2005.* Washington, DC: U.S. Department of Justice, Office of Justice Programs. Retrieved December 27, 2007, from http://www.ojp.usdoj.gov/bjs.

Bureau of Labor Statistics. (2006). *The survey of workplace violence prevention.* Washington, DC: U.S. Department of Justice, Office of Justice Programs. Retrieved November 10, 2006, from http://www.ojp.usdoj.gov/bjs.

Campbell, J. C., & Manganello, J. (2006). Changing public attitudes as a prevention strategy to reduce intimate partner violence. *Journal of Aggression, Maltreatment & Trauma, 13*(4), 13-40.

Campbell, J. C., Martin, S. L., Moracco, K. E., & Manganello, J., & Macy, R. J. (2006).
Survey data sets pertinent to the study of intimate partner violence and health.
Trauma, Violence and Abuse, 7, 3-18.

Carte, T. A., Chidambaram, L., & Becker, A. (2006). Emergent leadership in self-managed virtual teams. *Group Decision and Negotiations, 1*(10), 333-343.

Ceballo, R., Ramirez, C., Castillo, M., Caballero, G. A., & Lozoff, B. (2004). Domestic violence and women's mental health in Chile. *Psychology of women quarterly, 28,* 298-308.

Cherlin, J. A., Burton, M. L., Hurt, R.T., & Purvin, M. D. (2004). The influence of physical and sexual abuse on marriage and cohabitation. *American Sociology Review, 69,* 768-789.

Chronister, K. M. (2006). The intersection of social class and race in community intervention research with women domestic violence survivors. *American Journal of Community Psychology, 37*(3), 175-182.

Chronister, K. M. (2007). Contextualizing women domestic violence survivors' economic and emotional dependencies. *The American Psychologist, 62*(7), 706-708.

Chronister, K. M., & McWhirter, E. H. (2003). Women, domestic violence, and career counseling: An application of social cognitive career theory. *Journal of Counseling and Development, 81*(4), 418-424.

Chronister, K. M., & McWhirter, E. H. (2004). Ethnic differences in battered women's perceptions of career barriers and supports: A pilot study. *Journal of Career Assessment, 12*(2), 169-187.

Chronister, K. M., & McWhirter, E. H. (2006). An experimental examination of two career counseling programs for battered women. *Journal of Counseling Psychology, 53*, 151-164.

Chronister, K. M., Wettersten, K. B, & Brown, C. (2004). Vocational research for liberation of battered women. *Journal of Counseling Psychology, 32*, 900-922.

Chronister, K. M., Linville, D., & Palmer, K. (2008). Domestic violence survivors' access of career counseling services: A qualitative investigation. *Journal of Career Development, 34*, 339-361.

Chronister, K. M., Brown, C., O'Brien, K. M., Wettersten, K., B., Burt, M., Falkenstein, C., & Shahane, A. (2009). Domestic violence survivors. *Journal of Career Assessment, 17*(1), 116-131.

Cooper, D. R., & Schindler, P. S. (2008). *Business research methods* (10th ed.). Boston: McGraw-Hill.

Constantino, R.E., Kim, Y., & Crane, P.A. (2005). Effects of a Social Support Intervention on Health Outcomes: A pilot study. *Issues in Mental Health Nursing, 26*, 575-590.

Corporate Alliance to End Partner Violence. (2005). *Facts and statistics.* Retrieved November 14, 2006, from http://www.caepv.org.

Corporate Alliance to End Partner Violence. (2007). *Facts and statistics.* Retrieved February 7, 2009, from http://www.caepv.org.

Coulter, M. (2004). *Impact of domestic violence on the employment of women on welfare* (NCJ Publication No. 205294). Washington, DC: US Department of Justice, National Institute of Justice.

Creswell, J. W. (2007). *Educational research: Planning, conducting, and evaluating quantitative and qualitative research* (3rd ed). Upper Saddle River, NJ: Merrill-Prentice Hall.

Davies, L., Gilboe-Ford, M., & Hammerton, J. (2008). Gender inequality and patterns of abuse post leaving. *Journal of Family Violence, 24,* 27-39.

Dawson, R., & Huntington, N. (2004). *Secondary data analysis on the ethnology, course and consequences of intimate partner violence against extremely poor women.* (NCJ Publication No. 199714). Washington, DC: U.S. Department of Justice, National Institute of Justice.

Denning, S. (2005). Transformational innovation: A journey by narrative. *Strategy & Leadership, 33* (3), 11-16. Retrieved September 7, 2006, from ProQuest database.

Department of Health and Human Services. (2004). *Indicators of welfare dependence annual report to Congress 2004.* Retrieved November 28, 2006, http://www.ach.hhs.gov/news/stats/afdc.htm.

Department of Labor Women's Bureau. (2004). *Labor statistics.* Retrieved November 19, 2006, http://www.dol.gov/wb/faq38.htm.

Deprince, A., & Freyd, J. (2004). Forgetting trauma stimuli. *Psychological Science, 15,* 488-492.

Diop-Sidibé, N., Campbell, J. C., & Becker, S. (2006). Domestic violence against women in Egypt: Wife beating and health outcomes. *Social Science and Medicine, 62,* 1260-1277.

Duffy, M. K., Scott, K. L., & O'Leary-Kelly, A. M. (2005). The radiating effects of intimate partner violence on occupational stress and well-being. *Research in Occupational Stress and Well-Being, 4,* 30-57.

Encarta-Webster College Dictionary. (2nd ed.). (2005). New York: Bloomsbury Books.

Farmer, A., & Tiefenthaler, J. (2003). Explaining the recent decline in domestic violence. *Contemporary Economic Policy, 21,* 1-10. Retrieved May 19, 2005, from ProQuest database.

Fitzgerald, J. M., & Ribar, C. D. (2004). Welfare reform and female headship. *Demography, 41*(2), 189–212.

Fowler, D., & Hill, H. M. (2004). Social support and spirituality as culturally relevant factors in coping among African American women survivors of partner abuse. *Journal of Violence Against Women, 10*(11), 1267-1282.

Freire, P. (1970). *Pedagogy of the oppressed.* New York: Continuum.

Gielen, A., Campbell, J., Garza, M., O'Campo, P., Dienemann, J., Kub, J., Snow-Jones, A., & Lloyd, D. (2006). Domestic violence in the military: Women's policy preferences and beliefs concerning routine screening and mandatory reporting. *Military Medicine, 171* (8), 29-735.

Gondolf, E. W. (2005). *Culturally focused batterer counseling for African American men* (NCJ Publication No. 210828). Washington, DC: U.S. Department of Justice, National Institute of Justice.

Goodman, L., & Epstein, D. (2005). Refocusing on women: A new direction for policy and research on intimate partner violence. *Journal of Interpersonal Violence, 20*(4), 479-487.

Gorde, M. W., Helfrich, C. A., & Finlayson, M. L. (2004). Trauma symptoms and life skill needs of domestic violence victims. *Journal of Interpersonal Violence, 19*(6), 691-708.

Graen, G. B. (1976). Role-making process within complex organizations. In M. D. Dunnete (Ed.), *Handbook of industrial and organizational psychology* (pp. 1201-1245). Chicago: Rand McNally.

Gravetter, F. J., & Wallnau, L. B. (2005). *Essentials of statistics for the behavioral sciences* (5th ed.). Belmont, CA: Wadsworth/ Thomson Learning.

Green, S. G., & Mitchell, T. R. (1979). Attributional processes of leaders-member interactions. *Organizational Behavior and Human Performance, 23,* 429-458.

Hall-Haynes, I. (2003). Disclosure, intimate partner violence, and workplace assistance (Doctoral dissertation, Texas Women's

University, 2003). *UMI ProQuest Digital Dissertations*, No. 3084178.

Hamby, S., Sugarman, D., & Boney-McCoy, B. (2006). Does questionnaire format impact reported partner violence rates? An experimental study. *Violence and Victims, 21,* 1-9. Retrieved October 2, 2006, from ProQuest database.

Harland, L., Harrison, W., Jones, J. R., & Reiter-Palmon, R. (2005). Leadership behaviors and subordinates resilience. *Journal of Leadership & Organizational Studies, 11*(2), 1-10. Retrieved November 9, 2006, from ProQuest database.

Houghton, J. D., & Yoho, S. K. (2005). Toward a contingency model of leadership and psychological empowerment: When should self-leadership be encouraged? *Journal of Leadership & Organizational Studies, 11*(4), 65-83.

Hunter, D. Y., & Bandow, D. (2009). Abusive managers and variables impacting retaliation in organizations. *The Business Review, Cambridge, 12*(1), 32-39.

Johnson, M. (2006). Conflict and control: gender symmetry and asymmetry in domestic violence. *Violence Against Women, 12*(11), 1003-1018.

Johnson, P., & Indvik, J. (1999). The organizational benefits of assisting domestically abused employees. *Public Personnel Management, 28,* 1-8. Retrieved May 9, 2005, from ProQuest database.

Katula, S. (2006). Domestic violence in the workplace. Part I: Understanding how it affects victims. *AAOHN Journal, 54*(5), 1-6. Retrieved November 21, 2006, from ProQuest database.

Keashly, L. & Harvey, S. (2006). Workplace emotional abuse. In E. K. Kelloway, J. Barling & J. Furrell (Eds), *Handbook of Workplace Violence*. Thousand Oaks: Sage Publication.

Killas, M., Simonin, M., & De Puy, J. (2005). *Violence experienced by women in Switzerland over their lifespan: Results of the international violence against women survey (IVAWS)*. Berne: Stempfli.

Kirby, G. R., & Goodpaster, J. R. (2007). *Thinking* (4th ed.). Upper Saddle River, NJ: Prentice-Hall.

Koziol-McLain, J., Webster, D., McFarlane, J., Block, C. R., Ulrich, Y., Glass, N., & Campbell, J. C. (2006). Risk factors for femicide-suicide in abusive relationships: Results from a multi-site case control study. *Violence & Victims, 21,* 3-21.

Kwesiga, E., Bell, M. B., Pattie, M., & Moe, A. M. (2007). Exploring the literature on relationships between gender roles, intimate partner violence, occupational status, and organizational benefits. *Journal of Interpersonal Violence,22*(3), 312-326.

Landy, F. J. (2007). Review of the historical perspectives in industrial and organizational psychology. In L. Koppes (Ed), *Journal of the History of the Behavioral Sciences, 43*(4), 429-430.

Lee, S. J., & Vinokur, A. D. (2007). Work Barriers in the context of pathways to the employment of welfare-to-work clients. *American Journal Community Psychology, 40,* 301-312.

Leedy, P. D., & Ormrod, J. E. (2009). *Practical research: Planning and design* (9th ed.). New York: Prentice Hall.

Lent, R.W., Brown, S. D., & Hackett, G. (1994). Monograph: Toward a unifying social cognitive theory of career and academic interest, choice, and performance. *Journal of Vocational Behavior, 45,* 79-122.

Leone, J., Johnson, M., Cohan, C., & Lloyd, S. (2004). Consequences of male partner violence on low-income minority women. *Journal of Marriage and the Family, 66,* 472-490.

Lewis, J., Coursol, D., & Wahl, K. H. (2002). Addressing issues of workplace harassment: Counseling the targets. *Journal of Employment Counseling, 39,*109-117.

Lindhorst, T., Oxford, R., & Gillmore, M. R. (2007). Longitudinal effects on domestic violence on employment and welfare outcomes. *Journal of Interpersonal Violence, 22*(7), 812-828.

Lindley, L. (2005). Barriers to career development in the context of social cognitive career theory. *Journal of Career Assessment, 13,* 271-287.

Logan, T., Shannon, L., Cole, J., & Swanberg, J. (2007). Partner stalking and implications for women's employment. *Journal of Interpersonal Violence, 22*(3), 268-291.

Logan, T., & Walker, R. (2004). Separation as a risk factor for intimate partner violence victims: Beyond lethality and injury. *Journal of Interpersonal Violence, 19*(12), 1478-1486.

Luthans, F., & Avolio, B. J. (2003). Authentic leadership: A positive development approach. In K. S. Cameron, J. E. Dutton, & R. E. Quinn (Eds.), *Positive organizational scholarship* (pp. 241-258). San Francisco: Barrett-Koehler. Retrieved August 24, 2006, from Thompson-Gale PowerSearch database.

Luthans, F., Avolio, B. J., Walumbwa, F. O., & Li, W. (2005). The psychological capital of Chinese workers: Exploring the relationship with performance. *Management and Organization Review, 1*(2), 249-271.

Luthans, K. W., & Jensen, S. M. (2005). The linkage between psychological capital and commitment to organizational mission. *Journal of Nursing Administration, 35*(6), 304-310.

Luthans, F., & Youssef, C. M. (2007a). Positive workplaces. In C. R. Snyder, & S. Lopez (Eds.), *Handbook of Positive Psychology*. Oxford, UK: Oxford University Press.

Luthans, F., & Youssef, C. M. (2007b). Emerging positive organizational behavior. *Journal of Management, 33* (3), 321-349.

Luthans, F., Youssef, C. M., & Avolio, B. (2007a). *Psychological capital: Developing the Human Competitive Edge.* New York: Oxford University Press.

Luthans, F., Youssef, C. M., & Avolio, B. J. (2007b). Psychological capital: Investing and developing positive organizational behavior. In D. Nelson & C. L. Cooper (Eds.), *Positive organizational behavior: Accentuating the positive at work.* Thousand Oaks, CA: Sage

Lynham, S. A., & Chermack, T. J. (2006). Responsible leadership for performance: A theoretical model and hypotheses. *Journal of Leadership and Organizational Studies, 12*(4), 73-89.

Malhotra, N. K. (2004). *Marketing research: An applied orientation* (4ᵗʰ ed.). Prentice Hall, Upper Saddle, NJ.

Malhotra, N. K., Sung, S. S., & Patil, A. (2006). Common method variance in IS research: A comparison of alternative approach and reanalysis of past research. *Management Science, 52*(12), 1865-1883.

Masten, A. S., & Reed, M-G. J. (2002). Resilience in development. In C. R. Snyder & S. Lopez (Eds.), *Handbook of positive psychology* (pp. 74-88). Oxford, UK: Oxford University Press.

McCarthy, B., Felmlee, D., & Hagan, J. (2004). Girlfriends are better: Gender, friends and crime among school and street youth. *Criminology, 42,* 805-835.

McKean, L. (2004a). Addressing domestic violence as a barrier to work: Building collaborations between domestic violence provides and employment services agencies. *Center for Impact Research*, 1-16. Retrieved November 10, 2006, from ProQuest database.

McKean, L. (2004b). Self- sufficiency and safety: The case for onsite domestic violence services at employment service agencies. *Center for Impact Research*, 1-22. Retrieved November 10, 2006, from ProQuest database.

Mears, D. P., & Visher, C. A. (2005). Trends in understanding and addressing domestic violence. *Journal of Interpersonal Violence, 20*(2), 204-211.

Meltzer, S. (2002). Gender, work, and intimate violence: Men's occupational violence spillover and compensatory violence. *Journal of Marriage and the Family, 64,* 820-832.

Meglich, P. (2008). Gender effects of interpersonal workplace harassment. *The Journal of Applied Business and Economics, 8*(1), 9-15.

Meyer, S. (2004). Organizational response to conflict: Future conflict and work outcomes. *Social Work Research, 28,* 1-15. Retrieved May 9, 2005, from InfoTRAC database.

Moe, A., & Bell, M. (2004). Abject economics: The effects of battering and violence on women's work and employability. *Violence Against Women, 10*(1), 29-55.

Nam, Y. (2005). The roles of employment barrier in welfare exits and reentries after welfare reform: Event history analyses. *Social Service Review,* 269-291.

National Center for Injury Prevention and Control. (2003). *Costs of intimate partner violence against women in the United States.* Atlanta, GA: Centers for Disease Control and Prevention.

Nelson, D., & Cooper C. L. (2007). Positive organizational behavior: Accentuating the positive at work. Thousand Oaks, CA: Sage.

Neuman, B., & Fawcett, J. (2002). *The Neuman systems model.* Upper Saddle River, NJ: Prentice Hall.

Neuman, L. W. (2006). *Social research methods: Qualitative and quantitative approaches* (6th ed.). Sydney: Pearson Education.

Norman, S., Luthans, B., & Luthans, K. (2005). The proposed contagion effects of hopeful leaders on the resiliency of employees and organizations. *Journal of Leadership and Organizational Studies, 12,* 55-65.

Northouse, P. G. (2007). *Leadership theory and practices* (4th ed.). Thousand Oaks, CA: Sage.

Office of Violence Against Women. (2007). *About domestic violence.* Retrieved March 28, 2009, from http://www.ovw.usdoj.gov. htm.

Office of Texas General Counsel. (2009). *Summary of Accomplishments Annual Report FY 2008.* Retrieved December 16, 2009, from http://www.twc.state.tx.us.

Partnership for Public Service. (2007, June). *Training supervisors to be leaders: A missing element in efforts to improve federal performance.* Chicago. Retrieved December 21, 2010, from http://www.ourpublicservice.org/OPS/publications / viewcontentdetails.php ?id=11.

Pearce, C., Sims, H., Cox, J., & Ball, G. (2003). Trans actors, transformers and beyond: A multi-method development of a theoretical typology of leadership. *The Journal of Management Development, 22,* 1-22. Retrieved October 15, 2006, from ProQuest database.

Peterson, S. J., & Byron, K. (2008). Exploring the role of hope in job performance: Results from four studies. Journal of Organizational Behavior, *29*(6), 785-803.

Peterson, S. J., & Luthans, F. (2003). The positive impact and development of hopeful leaders. *Leadership and Organizational Development Journal, 24,* 26-31.

Poggenpoel, M. (2005). Obstacles in qualitative research: Possible solutions. *Education, 126*(2), 304-311.

Politis, D. (2004). Transformational and transactional leadership: Predictors of the stimulant determinate to creativity in organizational work environment. *Journal of knowledge management, 2,* 23-34.

Prilleltensky, I., & Nelson, G. (2002). *Doing psychology critically: Making a difference in diverse settings,* New York: Palgrave Macmillan.

Purvin, D. (2007). At the crossroads and in the crosshairs social welfare policy and low-income women vulnerability to domestic violence. *Social Problems, 54(2),* 1-16.

Rafferty, A. E., & Griffin, M. A. (2006). Refining individualized considerations: distinguishing developmental leadership and supportive leadership. *Journal of Occupational and Organizational Psychology,* 37-62. Retrieved August 24, 2006, from Thompson-Gale PowerSearch database.

Reeves, C., & O'Leary-Kelly, A. M. (2007). The effects and cost of intimate partner violence for work organizations. *Journal of Interpersonal Violence, 22*(3), 327-344.

Riger, S., & Staggs, S. (2004a). Welfare reform, domestic violence, and employment. *Violence Against Women, 10*(9), 961-990.

Riger, S., & Staggs, S. (2004b). *Impact of intimate partner violence on women's labor force participation* (NCJ Publication No.

207143). Washington, DC: US Department of Justice, National Institute of Justice.

Riger, S., Staggs, S. L., & Schewe, P. (2004). Intimate partner violence as an obstacle to employment among mothers affected by welfare reform. *Journal of Social Issues, 60,* 1-21. Retrieved May 9, 2006, from InfoTRAC database.

Romano, P. S. (2004). *Developing a research question.* Retrieved December 18, 2006, from http://som.ucdavis.edu/students/k30/folder.2004-06-1.4913658468/ 1DevelopingResearchQuest.ppt.

Schoorman, F. D., Mayer, R. C., & Davis, J. H. (2007). An Integrative Model of Organizational Trust: Past, Present and Future. *Academy of Management Review, 32*(2), 344-354.

Scott, W. R., & Davis, G. F. (2007). *Organizations and organizing: Rational, natural, and open systems.* Upper Saddle River, NJ: Prentice Hall.

Simons, T., Friedman, R., Liu, L. A., & McLean, P. J. (2007). Racial differences in sensitivity to behavior integrity: Attitudinal consequences, in-group effects, and trickle down among black and non-black employees. *Journal of Applied Psychology, 92*(3), 650-665.

Stark, E. (2006). Commentary on Johnson's conflict and control: gender symmetry and asymmetry in domestic violence. *Violence Against Women, 12* (11), 1019-1025.

Stephenson, C. (2004). Rebuilding trust: The integral role of leadership in fostering values, honesty, and vision. *Ivey Business Journal.* Retrieved September 8, 2006, from ProQuest database.

Strauser, D., Lustig, D., Cogdal, P., & Uruk, A. (2006). Trauma symptoms: Relationship with career thoughts, vocational identity, and developmental work personality. *The Career Development Quarterly, 54*(4), 1-9. Retrieved September 22, 2006, from ProQuest database.

Stringer, L. (2006). The link between the quality of the supervisor-employee relationship and the level of the employee's job satisfaction. *Public Organization Review, 6,* 125-142.

Swanberg, J. E., & Logan, T. K. (2005). Domestic violence and employment: A qualitative study. *Journal of Occupational Health Psychology, 10*, 3-17. Retrieved September 22, 2006, from EBSCOhost database.

Swanberg, J., & Logan, T.K. (2007). Intimate partner violence, employment, and the workplaces: An interdisciplinary perspective. *Journal of Interpersonal Violence, 22*(3), 263 267.

Swanberg, J., Macke, C., & Logan, T. K. (2005). Intimate partner violence, employment, and the workplace: Consequences and future directions. *Trauma, Violence, & Abuse, 4,* 1-26. Retrieved September 23, 2006, from ProQuest database.

Swanberg, J., Macke, C., & Logan, T. K. (2006). Intimate partner violence, women, and work: Coping on the job. *Violence and Victims, 21*(5), 561- 575.

Swanberg, J., Macke, C., & Logan, T. K. (2007). Working women make it work: Intimate partner violence, employment, and workplace support. *Journal of Interpersonal Violence, 22*(5), 292-311.

Taylor, M. J., & Barusch, A. S. (2004). Personal, family, and multiple barriers of long-term welfare recipients, *Social Work, 49*(2), 175-183.

Texas Health and Human Services Commission. (2007). *Fact sheet: Intimate partner violence in Texas.* Retrieved April 28, 2009, from http://www.hhsc.state.tx.us.

Thorndike, R. M., & Thorndike-Christ, T.T. (2009). Measurement and evaluation in psychology and education (8th ed.). Upper Saddle River, NJ: Prentice-Hall.

Tolman, R. M., & Wang, C. H. (2005). Domestic violence and women's employment: Fixed effects models of three waves of women's employment study data. *American Journal of Community Psychology, 36,*147-158.

Tucker, A., & Russell, F. J. (2004). The influence of the transformational leader. *Journal of Leadership & Organizational Studies, 10*(4), 103-116. Retrieved August 25, 2006, from Thompson-Gale PowerSearch database.

United States Equal Employment Opportunity Commission. (2009). *Statistic and Employment.* Retrieved December 10, 2009, from http://www.eeoc.gov.htm.

United States Government Accountability Office, Education, Workforce, and Income Security Division. (1998). *Domestic violence: Prevalence and implications for employment among welfare recipients* (Publication No. 99-12). Washington, DC: U.S. Government Printing Office.

Wettersten, K. B., Rudolph, S. E., Faul, K., Gallagher, K., Trangsrud, H. B., & Adams, K. (2004). Freedom through self-sufficiency: A qualitative examination of the impact of domestic violence on the working lives of women in shelter. *Journal of Counseling Psychology, 51,* 447-462.

Whitaker, D. J., Baker, C. K., Pratt, C., Reed, E., Suri, S., Pavlos, C. et al. (2007). A network model for providing culturally competent services for intimate partner violence and sexual violence. *Violence Against Women, 13*(2), 190-209.

Woods, S. J. (2005). Intimate partner violence and post-traumatic stress disorder symptoms in women: What we know and need to know. *Journal of Interpersonal Violence, 20*(4), 394-402.

Williams, K. L. & Mickelson, K. D. (2007). A psychological resource impairment model explaining partner violence and distress: Moderating role of income. *AM J Community Psychology, 40,* 13-25.

Yakushko, O., & Chronister, K. M. (2005). Immigrant women and counseling: The invisible others. *Journal of Counseling and Development, 83*(3), 292-298.

Yoshioka, M. R., & Choi, D. Y. (2005). Culture and interpersonal violence research: Paradigm shift to create a full continuum of domestic violence services. *Journal of Interpersonal Violence, 20*(4), 513-519.

Youssef, C. M. & Luthans, F. (2007). Positive organizational behavior in the workplace: The impact of hope, optimism, and resilience. *Journal of Management, 33*(5), 774-800.

Appendix A
Informed Consent: Permission to use Premises Form

UNIVERSITY OF PHOENIX

PERMISSION TO USE PREMISES, NAME, AND/OR SUBJECTS
(Facility, Organization, University, Institution, or Association)

Remington College, Houston Southeast

20985 Gulf Freeway, Webster, TX. 77573

X I hereby authorize Eric Smith, student of University of Phoenix, to use the premises (facility identified above) to conduct a study entitled: The Relationship Between Workplace Assistance and Interpersonal Workplace Harassment In Harris County, Texas.

X I hereby authorize, Eric Smith, student of University of Phoenix, to recruit subjects for participation in a conduct a study entitled: The Relationship Between Workplace Assistance and Interpersonal Workplace Harassment In Harris County, Texas.

X I hereby authorize Eric Smith, student of University of Phoenix, to use the name of the facility, organization, university, institution, or association identified above when publishing results from the study entitled: The Relationship Between Workplace Assistance and Interpersonal Workplace Harassment In Harris County, Texas

Signature _____   11/10/09

Date   11/12/09

Name: Dr. Mike Lanouette

Title Chief Academic Officer

85

Appendix B
Research Script

Good morning, afternoon, or evening

I am a doctoral candidate with the University of Phoenix-Online.

Thank you for giving this time to discuss your experiences. The purpose of this study is to determine if the types of workplace harassment from male partners relate to types of interpersonal workplace harassment from supervisors, co-workers, or a group of co-workers. Your participation in this current study is voluntary. If you choose not to participate or to withdraw from the current study at any time, you can do so without penalty or loss of benefit to yourself. The results of the current study will be used for publication, but your name will not be used, and your responses will be maintained in confidence. Do not put your place of employment, supervisor, co-workers, or a group of co-workers, name of harasser on any form.

In this research, there are no foreseeable risks to you. You will win a $150.00 gift certificate if your number is selected. Possible benefits of your participation are the information that you give will contribute to the body of knowledge and increase awareness of interpersonal harassment and its effects among employers and employees in the United States.

I would like to review the informed consent release form with you and answer any questions you may have concerning the form. Your identity will remain anonymous and confidential and information will not be disclosed to outside parties. Participants' identity (name) will not be used in the coding process or the current study. The informed consent form, which will include the participant's actual name will be kept in a safe and will be destroyed by fire after 3 years.

By signing the informed consent release form, you are expressing your willingness to participate in the current study. I am also signing the informed consent form agreeing to the confidentiality of your personal information. This session is scheduled for 20 to 30 minutes. Before I proceed with the questions, are you comfortable? Do you have any questions?

[Wait for Response]
[Go to informed consent form]

Appendix C
Informed Consent Form

Dear Research Participant,

I am a student at the University of Phoenix, working on a doctorate in organizational leadership in management. I am conducting a research study entitled The *Relationship between workplace harassment and interpersonal workplace harassment in Harris County, Texas*. The purpose of the current study is to determine if workplace harassment from male partners relate to interpersonal workplace harassment from supervisors, co-workers, or a group of co-workers. Your participation will involve giving me your demographical information, answering some questions, and filling out surveys. This should not take more than 20 to 30 minutes of your time. Your participation in this current study is voluntary. If you choose not to participate or to withdraw from the study at any time, you can do so without penalty or loss of benefit to yourself. The results of the current study will be used for publication, but your name will not be used, and your responses will be maintained in confidence. Do not put your place of employment, supervisor, co-workers, or a group of co-workers, name of harasser on any form.

In this research, there are no foreseeable risks to you. You will eligible win a $150.00 gift certificate if your number is randomly selected for participating in this current study. Although there are no direct benefits to you, possible benefits of your participation are that the information you give will contribute to the body of knowledge and increase awareness of interpersonal harassment and its effects among employers and employees in the United States.

As a participant of this research you should understand:

1. You may decline to participate or withdraw from participation at any time without consequences.
2. Your identity will be kept anonymous.
3. Eric Smith, the researcher, has thoroughly explained the parameters of the research study and all of my questions and concerns will be addressed.
4. Eric Smith, the researcher will structure a coding process to assure that anonymity of your name is protected.
5. Data will be stored in a metal safe and locked in a secured area. The data will be held for a period of three years, and then destroyed.

6.   The results of the current study will be used for publication.

If you have any questions concerning the current study, please call me by phone orally, at 210-380-4030 between 5:00 pm and 9:00 pm.

Thank you.

By signing this form I acknowledge that I understand the nature of the study, the potential risks to me as a participant, and the means by which my identity will be kept confidential and information will not be disclosed to outside parties. My signature on this form also indicates that I am 18 years or older and that I give my permission to voluntarily serve as a participant in the study described.

_____   _____
Research Participant Signature/Date   Researcher Signature/Date

Appendix D
Quantitative Data Analysis Agreement

Professional Statistical Services
2712 Gaston Gate
Mt. Pleasant, SC 29466
Voice: (843) 856 – 5102
Email: ProStatServices@earthlink.net

Professional Statistical Services Consulting Agreement

A. Introduction

This is an Agreement between:

Professional Statistical Services ("the Consultant"), which was established to provide research design, data collection, dataset building, statistical and psychometric analysis, litigation support, and editing of research and dissertation manuscripts to researchers, businesses, attorneys and their clients, and students.)

Professional Statistical Services has consented to provide its services to:

Eric Smith
San Antonio, Texas

("the Client") in the fields in which the Consultant has professional qualifications.

B. Confidentiality

1. The Consultant promises not to disclose, reveal or share any confidential or proprietary information about the Client, or the parties to whom the Client's data relates, except as required by law.

2. Any and all written confidential information disclosed pursuant to this Agreement shall be returned along with all copies of the same to the other party or shall be destroyed, upon request and at the option of the party that disclosed the confidential information.

3. The Consultant promises not to use or act on any confidential or proprietary information in a manner that would harm either the Client or clients of the Client, or deprive the Client, or any client of the Client, of current or potential business.

Effective date is as signed

Signed and dated by the parties hereto.

For Professional Statistical Services: For the Client:

_____   _____
Signature   Signature

President   _____
Title   Social Security Number/Federal Tax ID

January 3, 2011   _____
Date   Date

Appendix E
Instrument: Workplace Harassment Tool

1.	Have you worked/been employed during the last 3 months? If YES (1) to working	YES (1)	NO (2)	NA (66)
2.	Has your partner harassed you at work in person?	YES (1)	NO (2)	NA (66)
3.	Has your partner harassed you at work over the phone?	YES (1)	NO (2)	NA (66)
4.	Have you been late for work or left early because of any abuse?	YES (1)	NO (2)	NA (66)
5.	Have you missed work because of any abuse?	YES (1)	NO (2)	NA (66)
6.	Have you been reprimanded at work for behaviors related to any abuse (IPV)?	YES (1)	NO (2)	NA (66)
7.	Have you lost a job because of abuse (IPV)?	YES (1)	NO (2)	NA (66)
8.	Has your partner discouraged you from working?	YES (1)	NO (2)	NA (66)
9.	Has your partner prevented you from working? IF YES (1) to #9 (prevent from working, give some examples:	YES (1)	NO (2)	NA (66)

Appendix F
Interpersonal Workplace Dynamics Survey

INTERPERSONAL WORKPLACE DYNAMICS
(Individual responses are completely confidential...
your anonymity is guaranteed.)

The following survey is being conducted to investigate how various interpersonal workplace behaviors are evaluated by adults. If you decide to do this, you will be asked to participate in a survey lasting approximately ten to fifteen minutes. In an effort to protect your anonymity, in any report of this study, you will never be asked for your name.

If you participate in this project you will be furthering the education of a graduate student, as well as assisting in the exploration of an important topic in workplace behavior. The data will be incorporated into a project report submitted for a course requirement and will also be submitted to an appropriate scholarly journal. Taking part in this project is entirely up to you, and no one will hold it against you if you decide not to do it. If you take part, you may stop at any time.

<u>SECTION 1</u>

Please record your answers by filling in the blanks where requested or by circling the appropriate choice.

A. AGE: _____years and _____months
B. GENDER (circle only one):   (1) Female   (0) Male

C. RACE (circle only one):
    (1) Black (not Hispanic)
    (2) White (not Hispanic)
    (3) Hispanic
    (4) Asian
    (5) American Indian or Alaskan Native
    (6) Other

D. OCCUPATIONAL SETTING: (circle only one)

(1) Education
(2) Health Care
(3) Hospitality
(4) Manufacturing
(5) Administrative/Office
(6) Government
(7) Other_____

E. CURRENT JOB TITLE (please PRINT clearly):_____

F. TOTAL <u>PAID</u> WORK EXPERIENCE:____years and ____months.

G. Select the statement that **best** describes how much of the total paid work experience entered for the   previous question (Question F) was for full-time work (20 hours or more per week) or part-time work (less than 20 hours per week).

(1) All part-time
(2) Almost all part-time
(3) Slightly more part-time than full-time
(4) Equal part-time and full-time
(5) Slightly more full-time than part-time
(6) Almost all full-time
(7) All full-time

SECTION 2

Definition of Interpersonal Workplace Harassment (IWH): IWH refers to intentional and repeated, long-term behavior that is offensive, intimidating, abusive and humiliating. IWH behavior is directed at a target employee and threatens the target's job performance and physical and personal well being.

Instructions for Completing the Survey: Each of the 32 items listed below describes a workplace situation that might occur. You may notice that the situations described appear on the survey multiple times – with different people behaving in the manner described. Please keep in mind what the work relationship is between the employee and the person doing what is described. Assume that you are the employee in each situation and that the situation has gone on for over six months. Your answers should reflect YOUR opinions and experiences only.

For all 32 items, answer Parts 1, 2, and 3. First, decide whether the situation is an example of IWH (as IWH is defined at the beginning of Section 2) and answer Part 1. If your answer to Part 1 is "Yes", then rate the severity. Record your answers by circling the appropriate choice.

Your SUPERVISOR does the following behaviors for over six months:

Each of the items listed below describes a workplace behavior that might occur. Assume that you are the employee in each situation.
1. Determine whether or not you believe the situation represents Interpersonal Workplace Harassment.
2. For those behaviors that you judged to be interpersonal workplace harassment, rate the severity of each behavior from 1 (not severe at all) to 9 (as severe as it gets). If you answered "NO" to Part 1, DO NOT rate the severity of this behavior.

Behavior	Part 1 In your opinion, is this situation interpersonal workplace harassment?	Part2 Has this happened to you AT WORK?	Part 3 Have you done this to someone else AT WORK?
1. Your supervisor repeatedly and purposely excludes you from meetings that you need to attend in order to perform your job successfully. 1 2 3 4 5 6 7 8 9 not at somewhat moderately quite as severe all severe severe severe severe as it gets	NO YES	NO YES	NO YES
2. Your supervisor repeatedly blames you for mistakes for which you are not responsible. 1 2 3 4 5 6 7 8 9 not at somewhat moderately quite as severe all severe severe severe severe as it gets	NO YES	NO YES	NO YES
3. Your supervisor repeatedly yells at you, singles you out for angry outbursts and directs temper tantrums at you for no apparent reason 1 2 3 4 5 6 7 8 9 not at somewhat moderately quite as severe all severe severe severe severe as it gets	NO YES	NO YES	NO YES

5. Your supervisor repeatedly spreads hateful and malicious rumors about your personal life.

1	2	3	4	5	6	7	8	9
not at all severe		somewhat severe		moderately severe		quite severe		as severe as it gets

NO YES   NO YES   NO YES

6. Your supervisor routinely greets you in a pleasant and friendly manner whenever you run into one another during the workday.

1	2	3	4	5	6	7	8	9
not at all severe		somewhat severe		moderately severe		quite severe		as severe as it gets

NO YES   NO YES   NO YES

7. Your supervisor repeatedly takes credit for your ideas or results and fails to recognize and acknowledge your contributions.

1	2	3	4	5	6	7	8	9
not at all severe		somewhat severe		moderately severe		quite severe		as severe as it gets

NO YES   NO YES   NO YES

8. Your supervisor repeatedly and intentionally sabotages or steals your tools, equipment, supplies or work output.

1	2	3	4	5	6	7	8	9
not at all severe		somewhat severe		moderately severe		quite severe		as severe as it gets

NO YES   NO YES   NO YES

9. Your supervisor repeatedly withholds or refuses to provide information that you must have in order to perform your job successfully.

1	2	3	4	5	6	7	8	9
not at all severe		somewhat severe		moderately severe		quite severe		as severe as it gets

NO   YES   NO   YES   NO   YES

10. Your supervisor repeatedly makes aggressive or intimidating physical gestures such as pushing, slamming objects, finger pointing or glaring towards you.

1	2	3	4	5	6	7	8	9
not at all severe		somewhat severe		moderately severe		quite severe		as severe as it gets

NO   YES   NO   YES   NO   YES

11. Your supervisor routinely asks for and acknowledges your input on work-related matters.

1	2	3	4	5	6	7	8	9
not at all severe		somewhat severe		moderately severe		quite severe		as severe as it gets

NO   YES   NO   YES   NO   YES

12. Your supervisor repeatedly makes unreasonable work demands of you.

1	2	3	4	5	6	7	8	9
not at all severe		somewhat severe		moderately severe		quite severe		as severe as it gets

NO   YES   NO   YES   NO   YES

One CO-WORKER does the following behaviors for over six months:

Each of the items listed below describes a workplace behavior that might occur. Assume that you are the employee in each situation.
1. Determine whether or not you believe the situation represents Interpersonal Workplace Harassment.
2. For those behaviors that you judged to be interpersonal workplace harassment, rate the severity of each behavior from 1 (not severe at all) to 9 (as severe as it gets). If you answered "NO" to Part 1, DO NOT rate the severity of this behavior.

	Part 1 In your opinion, is this situation interpersonal workplace harassment?	Part2 Has this happened to you AT WORK?	Part 3 Have you done this to someone else AT WORK?
13. One co-worker repeatedly yells at you, singles you out for angry outbursts and directs temper tantrums at you for no apparent reason. 1 2 3 4 5 6 7 8 9 not at somewhat moderately quite as severe all severe severe severe severe as it gets	NO YES	NO YES	NO YES
14. One co-worker repeatedly takes credit for your ideas or results and fails to recognize and acknowledge your contributions. 1 2 3 4 5 6 7 8 9 not at somewhat moderately quite as severe all severe severe severe severe as it gets	NO YES	NO YES	NO YES
15. One co-worker repeatedly spreads hateful and malicious rumors about your personal life. 1 2 3 4 5 6 7 8 9 not at somewhat moderately quite as severe all severe severe severe severe as it gets	NO YES	NO YES	NO YES

101

16. One co-worker routinely greets you in a pleasant and friendly manner whenever you run into one another during the workday.

1	2	3	4	5	6	7	8	9
not at all severe		somewhat severe		moderately severe		quite severe		as severe as it gets

NO   YES   NO   YES   NO   YES

17. One co-worker repeatedly and purposely excludes you from meetings that you need to attend in order to perform your job successfully.

1	2	3	4	5	6	7	8	9
not at all severe		somewhat severe		moderately severe		quite severe		as severe as it gets

NO   YES   NO   YES   NO   YES

18. One co-worker routinely asks for and acknowledges your input on work-related matters.

1	2	3	4	5	6	7	8	9
not at all severe		somewhat severe		moderately severe		quite severe		as severe as it gets

NO   YES   NO   YES   NO   YES

19. One co-worker repeatedly makes aggressive or intimidating physical gestures such as pushing, slamming objects, finger pointing or glaring towards you.

1	2	3	4	5	6	7	8	9
not at all severe		somewhat severe		moderately severe		quite severe		as severe as it gets

NO   YES   NO   YES   NO   YES

20. One co-worker repeatedly blames you for mistakes for which you are not responsible.

1	2	3	4	5	6	7	8	9
not at all severe		somewhat severe		moderately severe		quite severe		as severe as it gets

NO YES   NO YES   NO YES

21. One co-worker repeatedly and intentionally sabotages or steals your tools, equipment, supplies or work output.

1	2	3	4	5	6	7	8	9
not at all severe		somewhat severe		moderately severe		quite severe		as severe as it gets

NO YES   NO YES   NO YES

22. One co-worker repeatedly withholds or refuses to provide information that you must have in order to perform your job successfully.

1	2	3	4	5	6	7	8	9
not at all severe		somewhat severe		moderately severe		quite severe		as severe as it gets

NO YES   NO YES   NO YES

A GROUP OF CO-WORKERS does the following behaviors for over six months:

	Part 1 In your opinion, is this situation interpersonal workplace harassment?	Part2 Has this happened to you AT WORK?	Part 3 Have you done this to someone else AT WORK?
Each of the items listed below describes a workplace behavior that might occur. Assume that you are the employee in each situation. 1. Determine whether or not you believe the situation represents Interpersonal Workplace Harassment. 2. For those behaviors that you judged to be interpersonal workplace harassment, rate the severity of each behavior from 1 (not severe at all) to 9 (as severe as it gets). If you answered "NO" to Part 1, DO NOT rate the severity of this behavior.			
23. A group of your co-workers repeatedly withholds or refuses to provide information that you must have in order to perform your job successfully. 1 2 3 4 5 6 7 8 9 not at somewhat moderately quite as severe all severe severe severe as it gets	NO YES	NO YES	NO YES
24. A group of your co-workers repeatedly makes aggressive or intimidating physical gestures such as pushing, slamming objects, finger pointing or glaring towards you. 1 2 3 4 5 6 7 8 9 not at somewhat moderately quite as severe all severe severe severe as it gets	NO YES	NO YES	NO YES
25. A group of your co-workers routinely greets you in a pleasant and friendly manner whenever you run into one another during the workday. 1 2 3 4 5 6 7 8 9 not at somewhat moderately quite as severe all severe severe severe as it gets	NO YES	NO YES	NO YES

26. A group of your co-workers repeatedly takes credit for your ideas or results and fails to recognize and acknowledge your contributions.

1	2	3	4	5	6	7	8	9
not at all severe		somewhat severe		moderately severe		quite severe		as severe as it gets

NO YES   NO YES   NO YES

27. A group of your co-workers repeatedly yells at you, singles you out for angry outbursts and directs temper tantrums at you for no apparent reason.

1	2	3	4	5	6	7	8	9
not at all severe		somewhat severe		moderately severe		quite severe		as severe as it gets

NO YES   NO YES   NO YES

28. A group of your co-workers repeatedly and intentionally sabotages or steals your tools, equipment, supplies or work output.

1	2	3	4	5	6	7	8	9
not at all severe		somewhat severe		moderately severe		quite severe		as severe as it gets

NO YES   NO YES   NO YES

29. A group of your co-workers repeatedly spreads hateful and malicious rumors about your personal life.

1	2	3	4	5	6	7	8	9
not at all severe		somewhat severe		moderately severe		quite severe		as severe as it gets

NO YES   NO YES   NO YES

105

										NO YES	NO YES	NO YES

30. A group of your co-workers repeatedly blames you for mistakes for which you are not responsible.

1	2	3	4	5	6	7	8	9
not at all severe		somewhat severe		moderately severe		quite severe		as severe as it gets

NO   YES   NO   YES   NO   YES

31. A group of your co-workers repeatedly and purposely excludes you from meetings that you need to attend in order to perform your job successfully.

1	2	3	4	5	6	7	8	9
not at all severe		somewhat severe		moderately severe		quite severe		as severe as it gets

NO   YES   NO   YES   NO   YES

32. A group of your co-workers routinely asks for and acknowledges your input on work-related matters.

1	2	3	4	5	6	7	8	9
not at all severe		somewhat severe		moderately severe		quite severe		as severe as it gets

NO   YES   NO   YES   NO   YES

Please review your survey to be sure that you have answered, Parts 1, 2, and 3 for EVERY question in Section 2. Your accurate and complete answers are greatly appreciated. Thank you for your time and thoughtful input.

Appendix G
Permission to use the Workplace Harassment Tool

UNIVERSITY OF PHOENIX

PERMISSION TO USE AN EXISTING SURVEY

January 31, 2007

Mr. Eric Smith
5534 Fredericksburg Road #242
San Antonio, TX

Thank you for your request for permission to use information from the United States Government Accountability Office's report entitled "Domestic Violence: Prevalence and Implications for Employment Among Welfare Recipients" (GAO-HEHS-99-12, Nov. 24, 1998). Because GAO's reports generally do not have copyrights in place, you do not need its permission to use or copy the information included in this report. This only applies to the GAO report. Note that this may not apply to studies cited in the report that you may have obtained.

Best wishes with your study.

Sincerely,

Gale C. Harris
Assistant Director, Education, Workforce and Income Security
United States Government Accountability Office

Appendix H
Permission to use Interpersonal
Workplace Dynamics Survey

UNIVERSITY OF PHOENIX

PERMISSION TO USE SURVEY INSTRUMENT

INTERPERSONAL HARASSMENT DYNAMICS SURVEY

I hereby authorize, Eric Smith, student of University of Phoenix, to use the survey mentioned above conduct a study entitled: THE RELATIONSHIP BETWEEN WORKPLACE ASSISTANCE AND INTERPERSONAL WORKPLACE HARASSMENT IN HARRIS COUNTY, TEXAS

Patricia Meglich

Signature

12/16/09

Date

Patricia Meglich, PhD, SPHR

Name

Title,

Assistant Professor of Management
University of Nebraska, Omaha